NEW MUSICAL RESOURCES

Henry Cowell

New Musical Resources

with notes and an accompanying essay by
David Nicholls

CAMBRIDGE
UNIVERSITY PRESS

Published by the Press Syndicate of the University of Cambridge
The Pitt Building, Trumpington Street, Cambridge CB2 IRP
40 West 20th Street, New York, NY 10011-4211, USA
10 Stamford Road, Oakleigh, Melbourne 3166, Australia

First Published 1930
This edition published 1996

Printed in Great Britain at the University Press, Cambridge

A catalogue record for this book is available from the British Library

Library of Congress cataloguing in publication data

Cowell, Henry, 1897–1965.
New musical resources / Henry Cowell; with notes and
an accompanying essay by David Nicholls
    p.   cm.
Includes index.

ISBN 0 521 49651 9 (hardback) – ISBN 0 521 49974 7 (paperback)
1. Music – Theory – 20th Century. 2. Harmonics (Music)
1. Nicholls, David, 1955 – . 11. Title.
MT6. C7895N4 1995
781. 2 – dc20   95–31529 CIP MN
ISBN 0 521 49651 9 hardback
ISBN 0 521 49974 7 paperback

Contents

NEW

MUSICAL RESOURCES

HENRY COWELL

NEW YORK · ALFRED·A·KNOPF · LONDON

MCMXXX

Contemporary music makes almost universal use of materials formerly considered unusable. These materials are in some degree acceptable to almost all music-lovers, and there is a tendency on the part of critics and the sophisticated public to be somewhat bored by new music which uses only old-fashioned means. In spite of their current use, however, little is known about the materials of contemporary music, and there are surprisingly few attempts to organize them into a unified system. Notwithstanding some very interesting works on new problems in music (such as Redfield's *Music: a Science and an Art*), written for the most part by scientists rather than musicians, a system co-ordinating the various materials of modern music has not been made public, so far as I know. Schönberg in his *Harmonielehre* carried the conventional study of harmony a step further. He explained many moderately complex harmonies by combining more chromatic passing tones and pointed out some well-known primary overtone relationships; but his work fails to explain music as involved as Schönberg's own compositions. A later theory, as yet unpublished by Schönberg, investigates very thoroughly the possibilities of the twelve-tone scale; which is, however, only one facet of contemporary materials.

ix

✿✿✿✿✿✿✿✿✿✿✿✿✿✿✿✿✿✿✿✿✿✿✿✿✿✿✿✿✿✿✿✿✿✿✿

Eaglefield Hull in his book *Modern Harmony* has made one of the few attempts to give a general explanation of modern phenomena. Hull did not, however, offer any theory as to why the particular materials actually in use should have been found more acceptable than many other means which might have been used in their place. Although Hull's book was written some years ago, his efforts in classifying musical means without giving reasons for their existence are reflected in the attitude of some musicians today. If a student is told that triads are built on intervals of a third, he is not thereby made aware of the entire system of conventional harmony. He not only must know why thirds are acceptable materials for building triads, but must study the details of chord-connexion, perhaps for years, to gain a knowledge of their handling. Similarly, to state that a certain chord in modern music is built up in fourths is not a sufficient explanation. A reason for the suitability of fourths as building-material must be shown, as well as some idea of the practical problems to be overcome in connecting fourth chords, before any knowledge of such chords is gained.

The purpose of *New Musical Resources* is not to attempt to explain the materials of contemporary music, many of which are not included in its discussion, but to point out the influence the overtone series has exerted on music throughout its history, how many musical materials of all ages are related to it, and how, by various means of applying its principles in many different manners, a large palette of musical materials can be assembled. Some of them are in use, some of them are presaged in contemporary music, and some of them seem to be unused so far. Whether such materials are or are not in use it is not the purpose to discover; rather the purpose is to show the co-ordination of all possible musical materials within a certain overtone radius, regardless of whether they are yet in actual use. The very fact that such materials are built on the overtone series, which is the greatest factor in musical relationship, shows that they probably have potential musical use and value. That many of them remain as yet unused or only very tentatively suggested, makes the field which is opened up all the richer.

The result of a study of overtones is to find the importance of relationships in music and to find the measure by which every interval and chord may be related. It is discovered that the sense of consonance, dissonance, and discord is not fixed, so that it must be immovably applied to certain combinations, but is relative. It is also discovered that rhythm and tone, which have been thought to be entirely separate musical fundamentals (and still may be considered so in many ways) are definitely related through overtone ratios. Therefore the theory proposed may be termed a theory of musical relativity.

Incidentally, one of the results of an examination into the application of overtone relationships is to discover a way of logically co-ordinating many seemingly chaotic materials used in contemporary music, so that without that being its purpose, *New Musical Resources* throws an illumination on some difficult problems of "modernism," and shows that much "modern" music is not proceeding blindly. This is not always true, of course, as in many cases it suffers from a lack of knowledge by the composer of the materials used; and there is without question much inconsistency of texture to be found in some contemporary composition.

The aim of any technique is to perfect the means of expression. If a technique serves to dry up and inhibit the expression, it is useless as technique. Leaving the means of expression imperfect, however, does not solve the problem. Hearing innumerable passages in contemporary music which it is evident could be improved by the changing of a few mistaken notes (not to conform to some preconceived standard, but to express more consistently the composer's own idea) makes one wish that there could be more precision in the choice of notes, more intellectual understanding of each particular harmonic connexion. It may be felt that this work is done in the study of conventional harmony. Harmony as it is taught, however, contains discrepancies. Some of its rules are based on underlying science and more inevitable principles, but many other rules, inextricably mixed with the necessary ones, are based on the taste of a former era of music and are subject to change. Perhaps because these empirical rules have little application to problems of contemporary music, there has

❀❀❀❀❀❀❀❀❀❀❀❀❀❀❀❀❀❀❀❀❀❀❀❀❀❀❀❀❀

been on the part of some a reaction against the idea that knowledge of musical materials is necessary. Now, however, it is generally conceded that ignorant daring in the use of new materials results in many childish crudities and is often accompanied by absence of musical invention. It is therefore of interest to make public a system showing the relationship and use of contemporary materials. The aim in suggesting new materials is not, of course, to have them supersede old ones, but rather to supplement them, as well as adding new resources to the entire tonal palette.

Because the present work is not an attempt to explain the methods of specific composers, no quotations have been taken from actual compositions, but all necessary examples have been specially constructed to illustrate the various points.

A discussion of different sorts of temperament, or tuning, has not been attempted, as it has been assumed that the tones of the overtone series, being unconsciously if not consciously heard whenever a single tone is sounded, are a natural criterion. Therefore all temperaments from this point of view may be considered as an attempt to solve the problem of making some of the overtone relationships practical for musical use. In order to do this it has been necessary to alter the relationships slightly in various ways, by equalizing minute differences, etc. But it seems probable that a keen auditor has suggested to him through his musical imagination the overtone relationship nearest to the very close equivalents of the different modes of temperament, of which some are closer than others to the original series. Differences of temperament, however, and practical methods for making them possible on musical instruments, form a fascinating subject. Divisions of the octave into mathematically equal parts form the basis for the scales in much music. Javanese music divides the octave into five equal parts; Siamese music uses a scale of nine equal divisions of the octave. The whole-tone scale as used by Debussy and others divides the octave into six parts. Our own keyboard instruments divide the octave into twelve parts, and Schönberg bases his new theoretical system on such a division. The quarter-tone scale as proposed by Alois Hába and others would divide the octave into twenty-four equal steps. These divisions are not unrelated to the overtone series, as the intervals they form can be found among overtone relationships. Other systems of temperament more immediately related to the overtone series deal with unequal or diatonic divisions of the octave. Interest in differences of temperament comes largely through consideration of scales. In this work it is suggested that scales as well as other aspects of music are related to the overtone series, which is a scale in its upper reaches, a harmony in its lower reaches, and a basis for rhythmical co-ordination.

It is not the aim of this work to delve into questions of æsthetics, into any philosophical discussion of what

is good or bad, what should or should not be done, or
what may or may not be done. These are questions
which are answered by the dictates of taste, and taste
and fashions in taste change. It is my conviction, however, that the finest taste and the perfect use of scien-
tifically co-ordinated materials go together, and that the
musical resources outlined add to the possibilities of
musical expression and are therefore vital potentialities,
rather than merely cold facts.

My interest in the theory underlying new materials
came about at first through wishing to explain to my-
self, as well as to others, why certain materials I felt
impelled to use in composition, and which I instinctively felt to be legitimate, have genuine scientific and
logical foundation. I therefore made an investigation
into the laws of acoustics as applied to musical materials. Some of the results of the investigation convinced me that although my music itself preceded the
knowledge of its theoretical explanation, there had
been enough unconscious perception so that the means
used were not only in accordance with acoustical law,
but are perhaps the best way of amalgamating sounds
formerly considered discords; namely, by sounding together a number of tones related through the higher
reaches of the overtones, in the same spacing in which
they occur in the overtone series. Some of the results of
this probing into acoustical relationships form the basis
for this work.

✾✾✾✾✾✾✾✾✾✾✾✾✾✾✾✾✾✾✾✾✾✾✾✾✾✾✾✾✾✾✾✾✾✾✾✾

It will readily be seen that the various fields opened up are merely suggested, and that a separate book would have to be written about each one of the subjects, such as polyharmony, polyrhythm, or tone-cluster, to make any detailed application of the principles shown. There are primary subjects other than those treated of here to which the same general method of procedure might be applied, opening up other new fields; and by applying the same process of development to a study of the possibilities of combining the primary elements dealt with in this work, a further extension may be made.

New Musical Resources was first written during 1919, with the literary assistance of Professor Samuel S. Seward, of Stanford University, to whom I am deeply indebted. In this early form it embraced most of the applications given here of the theory of musical relativity. Many of the materials which it predicted would come into music have since been adopted; many materials which were only vaguely suggested in music at the time, and which were pointed out as valid, have since been developed to such an extent that it is difficult to realize with what suspicion they were regarded in 1919. For example, the chapter on dissonant counterpoint was at that time a proposal that such a counterpoint be formulated. Since then Ruggles and Hindemith have been heralded as apostles of dissonant counterpoint, and Schönberg has brought to a clear focus the counterpoint which was a mere suggestion in his opus 11 and other works of an earlier period. Similar developments have been made in many of the branches treated. Such progress is encouraging and seems to give further proof that the theory as postulated has validity.

PART I

Tone Combinations

✺✺✺✺✺✺✺✺✺✺

1. *The Influence of Overtones in Music*

The reason for reviewing certain scientific and historical aspects of music is not to bring out new facts, but to present these facts in a new light, and to seize and emphasize certain salient ideas which there will be occasion to apply, and which are necessary to the understanding of what follows; for while the musical public may be familiar with the idea that our musical materials have undergone a change from simple to more complex during musical history, it is apt to be a general and rather vague notion, rather than one about which many particular facts are known; and comparatively few know how closely the history of harmony has followed the series of natural overtones. Many musicians know the intervals produced by the lower members of the overtone series, but few have considered all the different aspects of the relationships formed by them, or have studied higher overtone relationships.

Music is based upon, and conditioned by, the physical laws of sound-waves. These laws disclose that musical tones have a relation to each other which is measurable by mathematics. They further show that each tone produced generates a series of overtones

3

which are related to that tone, and to each other, by definite mathematical ratios. These overtones stretch upwards indefinitely. Our ear can follow them a certain distance; instruments can follow them further yet; but the theoretical range of them is beyond our power to follow. On many instruments, such as the piano, the whole series as far as the ear can follow is present in almost equally graduated shades, the lowest being most easily heard, the higher ones growing gradually dimmer and dimmer. On some instruments, owing to their construction, certain overtones are lacking or very dim, while others are more prominent. Such differences are the means of giving individuality of tone-quality to different instruments.

Experiment has shown that if the fundamental tone be removed altogether, leaving only overtones sounding, we are so accustomed to associating the sound of these overtones with a single sound that the series of overtones alone still sounds like a single tone to us, and we think we are hearing the fundamental tone, with rather a thin quality.

Ancient instruments were not nearly so rich in overtones as our modern ones, and it is perhaps for this reason that only the simple major triad, formed by some of the lower reaches of the overtone series, was formerly regarded as a "natural" chord. On present-day instruments the higher overtones, as well as the lower ones, are so easily heard that the ear cannot help being aware, when a single tone is played, of sounds which

4

would formerly have been called discords. Professor Dayton Miller, well-known acoustician and author of *The Science of Musical Sound,* speaks of having heard the forty-fourth overtone with his unaided ear. A number of experiments on the piano are possible which serve to show how distinctly some of the higher overtones may be heard. For example, if the notes B, D, F, A flat are pressed down without sounding, and then the notes C, E flat, G flat, A are played sharply staccato, without pedal, the sound which will remain is a complex of higher and more dissonant overtones.

Since the higher overtones are so readily heard on our modern instruments, it is evident that they have a strong influence, unconsciously if not consciously, on what we can regard as acceptable harmonic combinations; and we shall be much more apt to react musically to a new dissonance if it is one which follows natural overtone complexes, and is therefore within the experience of the listener who has heard it as overtones of some simple combination, than if it has no close relation to the overtones. Therefore it would seem that the overtones should be made the basis of musical theory to a far greater extent than they have been, and that in particular the new types of chords found in contemporary music might be studied in relation to higher overtone combinations. Thus whenever the familiar chord C, G, E is struck, the overtones of all three of these tones are perceivable to the ear. Without going further than the first four overtones we arrive at the

5

❀❀❀❀❀❀❀❀❀❀❀❀❀❀❀❀❀❀❀❀❀❀❀❀❀❀❀❀❀❀❀❀

following chord: C, E, G, G sharp, B, D; if we take the first six overtones, we arrive at the following chord: C, E, G, G sharp, B flat, B, D, F. This method of investigation should prove of interest and benefit and is heartily recommended to anyone wishing to work out the details.

The manner in which the overtone series is generated is as follows: A string or other sound-producing medium on being tapped, scraped, or otherwise set into vibration first vibrates (or oscillates) as a whole, producing the fundamental tone. The string, however, does not stop with vibrating as a whole. Of its own accord, without any added outside persuasion, it begins vibrating in two equal sections, so that the vibration is divided at the centre of the string, which is comparatively still. This vibration in halves is twice as fast as the fundamental vibration and produces a tone an octave higher, which is called the first overtone. The vibration in halves does not cancel the original vibration as a whole, but is superimposed upon it; and it should be noted that all higher overtones are in the same way added to the vibration of the string, without interfering with any of the other overtones, which all continue to sound together; although at times when the vibration curves clash, parts of the sound may be blotted out periodically. After subdividing into halves, the string then divides itself into three equal sections, each of which produces a so-called second overtone, which is an octave and a fifth higher than the fundamental, and which is produced by each third of the length of the string vibrating three times as fast as the fundamental. The string then continues to subdivide itself into fourths, fifths, sixths, sevenths, etc., *ad infinitum;* or until the string stops vibrating, or unless some impediment in the string stops or deflects the series. It will be noted that the first overtone is sounded twice, once by each half of the string, at the same moment; the second overtone is sounded three times, once by each third of the string, etc.

The following chart of overtones brings out all the points that need so far to be understood.

In the first column the major scale is written from the fundamental C up to and including the third octave above. It is convenient to close the chart at this point. In actuality higher octaves succeed each other indefinitely.

The second column shows to which tone of the scale these overtones correspond. Up to the seventh tone, it will be observed, no recourse is had to either sharps or flats.

The third column gives the names of the intervals thus created, beginning with the octave, the fifth, etc. As the tones go higher in the series, the intervals become successively smaller.

The next column indicates the relative vibration speed of each tone of the overtone series. That is, if the fundamental C is caused by 16 vibrations each second of time, the next higher C, or the octave, will

Notes of Major Scale (Read up.)	Overtone Notes	Intervals	Vibration Index (on base of 16)	Serial Numbers of Partials *
c.......	C	Large major second	128 = 8(16)	8
b				
	(B♭)	Small minor third	112 = 7(16)	7
a				
g.......	G	Minor third	96 = 6(16)	6
f				
e.......	E	Major third	80 = 5(16)	5
d				
c.......	C	Perfect fourth	64 = 4(16)	4
b				
a				
g.......	G	Perfect fifth	48 = 3(16)	3
f				
e				
d				
c.......	C	Perfect octave	32 = 2(16)	2
b				
a				
g				
f				
e				
d				
c.......	(Fundamental C, generating overtones)		16 = 1(16)	1

* The fundamental C and its series of overtones form the series of partials.

have 32 vibrations to the second, the next higher G 48 vibrations, and so on up through the series. The number of vibrations of each overtone will be an exact multiple of 16, and the coefficients will mount in uninterrupted regularity—2 (times 16), 3, 4, 5, etc. It will be noted that the overtone series includes each

✿✿✿✿✿✿✿✿✿✿✿✿✿✿✿✿✿✿✿✿✿✿✿✿✿✿✿✿✿✿✿✿✿✿✿✿

C that appears in the higher reaches of the scale. More than that, the vibration speed of each successively higher C increases in geometrical progression, 2 times, 4 times, 8 times, 16. Since, then, the vibration speed between octaves rises with increasing rapidity in geometrical progression, whereas the vibration speed between overtones rises steadily in arithmetical progression, it is evident that more and more intervals are included within each higher octave, and the intervals themselves become proportionately smaller. An examination of the chart shows that this is just what happens. The principle can be applied beyond the limits of the chart as here given; thus, since there is but one interval in the lowest octave, two intervals in the second, and four in the third, it follows that there must be eight in the fourth octave, should the chart be extended to include that also. (See chart, page 11.)

That the overtones in that higher octave must come closer and closer together follows as a matter of course.

The last column gives the serial numbers by which the partials may be designated. Here the important fact to be observed is that any given number indicates, not only its position relative to the fundamental tone, but also the number by which 16 must be multiplied in order to give the vibration speed of that tone. Thus, the fifth tone of the series is caused by 5 times 16 ($= 80$) vibrations to each second of time.

Considered as a matter of musical practice, if we combine overtone relationships into chords, it is found

9

that the ear has accepted most readily such combinations as are made by the lower tones of the series. Combinations so accepted are known as simple or consonant chords. As tones higher in the series are incorporated into chords, the effect increases in complexity, and the ear accepts less and less readily, until a point is reached where the ear fails to rest satisfied with the resultant chord, and what is known as dissonance begins. If in a given dissonant chord the shifting of the tone causing dissonance to a step next lower, or by certain other methods, restores the chord to what seems consonant harmony, the dissonance is said to be resolved. Dissonant tones, then, are those for which the ear, in a certain state of musical development, demands resolution. What has been called discord results either when still higher overtone relationships are formed into chords, or when the tones of a dissonant chord are so spaced that the possibility of resolution is not suggested to the ear.

It is a notable fact that certain combinations accepted as satisfactory by one listener are found to be unsatisfying to another, and this acceptance or rejection of a given chord depends very largely upon the familiarity of the ear with the chord in question—that is to say, upon the musical experience of the listener. The points in the series, therefore, where consonant chords leave off and dissonance begins, and where dissonance leaves off and discord begins, are not rigidly fixed, as was assumed by most theorists, but depend upon the ear of the particular listener, who is in turn influenced by the musical age in which he lives. It is this fact, proved by the history of musical progress, in conjunction with the fact that, acoustically speaking, there is no point at which any other than an arbitrary difference between them can be shown, which establishes the relativity of consonance, dissonance, and discord.

Notes of Scale	Overtone Notes	Intervals	Vibration Index (on base of 16)		Serial Numbers of Partials
c......C		Small minor second	256	16(16)	16
b......B		Large minor second	240	15(16)	15
	(B♭)	Second	224	14(16)	14
a	(A♭)	"	208	13(16)	13
g......G		"	192	12(16)	12
f	(F♯)	"	176	11(16)	11
e......E		Small major second	160	10(16)	10
d......D		Large major second	144	9(16)	9
c......C			128	8(16)	8

(This chart is a continuation of the previous chart, carried an octave higher. Tones in parentheses do not exactly coincide in pitch with the tones of our present scale system.)

In other words, there is no greater difference between a minor third, with a vibration ratio of 5:6 (the most complex interval to be termed a concord in text-books), and a sub-minor seventh, with a ratio of 4:7 (the simplest interval to be termed a dissonance), than there is between the same interval of a minor third and the interval of a major sixth, with a ratio of 3:5, both of which are classed as concords by custom.

Looking back over the history of music, it must be admitted that we have no means of knowing exactly what was done by the very ancient peoples; there is some evidence, however, to support the theory that in ancient Greece the great choruses sang in unison, using no harmony whatsoever, and that the instruments which accompanied the choruses also simply played the melody with the voices. There are references to the lack of musicality on the part of any singer who sang notes apart from the body of the chorus.

A melody with percussion accompaniment but no harmony is characteristic of nearly all primitive music.

In early ecclesiastical music, when an attempt was made to revive early Greek modes, only melody alone was at first used, even as a priest chants the mass. Octaves, however, seem to have been accepted without question. Why octaves? Because the musicians of that time accepted instinctively an interval that science demonstrates to be, measured by rapidity of vibration, in the simple ratio of 1:2. The next interval to be accepted as harmonious by the ecclesiastics, after a long battle among theorists as to whether it was a discord introduced by the Devil to spread discontent, was the fifth; and this, as shown by the chart, relates itself to the octave by the ratio of 2:3 (or to the fundamental by the ratio of 1:3), the next simplest ratio. The next ratio, of 1:4, brought the available tones to the second octave, an obvious step, but by combination with former materials the new ratio 3: 4, producing the interval of a fourth, was obtained. The next tone which the ear found could be agreeably joined to the intervals of the octave and the fifth and fourth was the third above the second octave, and these two tones are found to be related in the ratio of 4: 5. With C as a base, the different tones thus far combined prove to be C, G, and E; in other words, the familiar "common chord," or tonic triad. The interval of a third when first introduced was considered a discord, then a dissonance demanding resolution. Only after many centuries was it freely permitted as a concord.

Enough has now been said to make clear the significance of musical progress in its earlier stages. Each step in historical progress was marked by an innovation—the use of one or more overtone relationships in combination with the tone combinations already accepted. Each innovation was felt at the time to be both radical and daring, and as such it was resisted until the musical ear of the period, grown accustomed to the new combination, accepted it as essentially consonant or "harmonious." It is a striking fact that chords and intervals accepted today as exceedingly simple, such as the common chord, were at one time felt to be complex to the point of discord.

From these beginnings music has proceeded steadily in the same direction. Many increasingly complex intervals have been added, at first as passing or auxiliary tones, then as part of a chord demanding resolution, and finally, as the ear became more and more used to them, as independent chord tones, without specific obligation. Each one of these intervals was, when it was added, the one formed by the next highest members of the overtone series, following those already in use. The composers who added new intervals, or new uses of old ones, were considered dangerously extreme; now most of them are accepted as leading masters of their time. We are apt to overestimate greatly the acceptance of such composers in their own day, because we read so much in musical history of the many followers who did appreciate and herald them. These followers, however, were only too often very much in the minority; and by reading the actual press-notices of the time, one discovers that critics as well as the public in general strongly resisted any attempts to introduce new musical material, which, nevertheless, was used in spite of them by strong-willed composers and became the very standard of acceptance by the critics and public of the next generations.

It has become popular to assert that most great composers were accepted fully in their own time, and that many of them did not introduce new material. Reading actual records, however, we find that Monteverdi was ridiculed for his unresolved and unprepared sevenths and his *tremolando* on the stringed instruments. Bach was called crude because of his enharmonic double dissonant passing tones, in which he used the melodic minor scale both ascending with sharped sixth and seventh degrees, and descending with natural sixth and seventh degrees at the same time. Mozart wrote a whole-tone-scale passage, and ended one of his works in four keys at once. Beethoven began his First Symphony on a dissonance which is out of the main key of the movement and was soundly berated for doing so by the most important critics of his day. Beethoven's many innovations of form and his free use of unresolved dissonances were understood by very few. Most admired were some of his earlier works which did not deviate from Mozartian form; Hummel, however, was almost universally considered to be the greatest living composer in Beethoven's own time. Wagner's addition of free use of ninth chords, as well as secondary seventh chords and accented appoggiaturas, gained him the reputation of being entirely incomprehensible, and his music was said to contain neither melody, harmony, nor form. By the time Wagner's music found acceptance, Debussy, by his development of the whole-tone scale, and the free use of seconds, was the composer who was considered utterly strange and without meaning. Now most music-lovers find Debussy musical, but have more recent pet aversions.

It would be difficult to state exactly where the first instance of any particular interval or some specific use of it actually occurs. Thus, although Debussy is given credit for the use of the whole-tone scale, instances of its sporadic use may be found in Mozart, Liszt,

Moussorgsky, and others. Nevertheless, Debussy developed the use of this scale far beyond the conception of anyone who had gone before, nor can it be said that the whole-tone scale had a serious position in music until he had shown its various uses. The same is true of most intervals. It may be very difficult to decide when they were first used, but their first important and consistent use can nearly always be identified with some one composer, and their period in musical history can be said to be his period.

It is interesting to observe that as musicians became accustomed to reach into the higher ranges of the overtone series for their harmonic material, there was a corresponding tendency to reject the simplest ratios, 1:2 (octaves), 2:3 (fifths), and 3:4 (fourths), as harmonically insipid and undesirable; and rules still govern their use such as are applied to no other intervals except dissonant and discordant ones.

There is a distinction to be drawn between making use of a new overtone in harmony, and fully assimilating that tone into older harmonic material. For example, two tones used together in a new interval may be justified both mathematically, as related tones of the overtone series, and to the ear, as a not inacceptable dissonance. But the new interval, if combined freely with several other tones in the series, may give an effect markedly dissonant, if not discordant. What is called the "spacing" of tones, or the choice of octaves in which given tones are used, has also its effect upon the ac-

16

✿ ✿

ceptability of a given combination, since it changes the ratio between the tones in question. Thus, the interval of a major seventh within the octave has a ratio of 8:15, whereas if it were spaced three octaves and a seventh apart, the ratio would be 1:15. Since this ratio contains no beats, but, on the contrary, the vibrations are periodically even, it is questionable whether the interval of a major seventh can be called dissonant when in this spacing. A field of interesting investigation is opened up by a consideration of similar instances of distinctions between intervals which have been called by the same name, according to how many octaves apart their component tones are placed.

Innovation, then, may be of two kinds—both reaching a step higher into the range of overtones for musical material, and using the material thus gained in a greater variety of tone combinations. For example, Schönberg has developed a certain set of intervals and more or less perfected the use of them; but there is no reason why men like Hindemith and Alban Berg should not be called innovators when they discover new possible combinations of Schönberg's material with older means already at hand.

Another point to be observed grows out of the demonstrated fact that as overtones go higher and higher in the series, the tones come closer and closer together. The musical scale that we use provides for intervals as close together as half-tones, but beyond a certain point —namely, the sixteenth partial—tones closer together than the half-tone that we use, for which our scales do not provide, are generated by the overtone series. Successful experiments, and the well-known practice of Oriental music, show that these tones are not beyond the capacity of the human ear.

Professor Leon Theremin in a demonstration of his electrical instruments, showed that the interval of one-hundredth part of a whole step can be plainly discerned by an audience. The probabilities are that any intervals which are perceivable as distinct to the human ear can find musical use in some form and under certain circumstances. The term "quarter-tones" has become a byword for any mention of intervals less than a half-step, partly because it is physically easier to construct instruments capable of producing quarter-tones than most other values, as they fall just half-way between the half-tones on any keyboard instrument. Many composers have used quarter-tones in their works. There is a quarter-tone piano in the conservatory of Moscow which was built in 1864, and Georg Rimsky-Korsakoff has worked with quarter-tones more recently in Russia. Charles Ives in America has been using them for many years. At the National Conservatory in Prague a department for quarter-tones is conducted by Alois Hába, who has done a great deal for their advancement. He has developed a notation which takes into consideration their enharmonic shades and has used them not sporadically but consistently in his

❀❀❀❀❀❀❀❀❀❀❀❀❀❀❀❀❀❀❀❀❀❀❀❀❀❀❀❀❀❀❀❀

compositions and has investigated them acoustically. Hába has also investigated the many intervals which occur in the overtone series between the half- and quarter-tones. This seems an important consideration, because while these intervals are almost unknown and have no specific names among musicians, they are the next in the overtone series from the ones we now use in our music; and, as music has since its early history progressed directly up the overtone series, there is a strong possibility that the next development may be to add to music the next highest overtone after the half-step, our present most complex interval. This would not give the quarter-step, but an interval a little smaller than a half-step. The half-step is a 15:16 ratio; the quarter-step is a 30:31 ratio. Therefore it would seem that the quarter-step is not the next interval for use, from an acoustical or historical standpoint, but has been regarded as such only because of the mechanical ease of dividing the half-step exactly in half. Theremin's instruments may make it possible to play the intervening and acoustically simpler intervals with as great ease as quarter-tones; thus one of the main difficulties, that of performance, can be solved.

Sliding tones, based on ever-changing values of pitch instead of steady pitches, are sometimes used in music. Such tones are very frequently used in primitive music, and often in Oriental music; in our music they are rarer, and a very frequent use has been considered in bad taste. They have been largely a matter of performance rather than composition, as there is no clearly defined method of notating them.

Natural sounds, such as the wind playing through trees or grasses, or whistling in the chimney, or the sound of the sea, or thunder, all make use of sliding tones. It is not impossible that such tones may be made the foundation of an art of composition by some composer who would reverse the programmatic concept, such as expounded by Richard Strauss. Instead of trying to imitate the sounds of nature by using musical scales, which are based on steady pitches hardly to be found in nature, such a composer would build perhaps abstract music out of sounds of the same category as natural sound—that is, sliding pitches—not with the idea of trying to imitate nature, but as a new tonal foundation.

Sliding tones do not seem to have specific connexion with overtones, and are mentioned here to indicate the possibility of musical systems derived otherwise than from overtones. It is difficult to find musical means to which overtones do not apply, or may not be applied, as they may be used to measure all relationships of steady pitch, no matter how subtle are the degrees of pitch chosen; and all rhythmical relationships can be derived from overtones, as will be shown. Even in sliding pitch, if several parts move against each other, the tonal relationship at any particular instant may be measured by the overtone series, and if sliding tones

✸✸✸✸✸✸✸✸✸✸✸✸✸✸✸✸✸✸✸✸✸✸✸✸✸✸✸✸✸✸✸

are used as passing-notes between two steady pitches (as in Hawaiian music), the distance covered by the slide is a matter for overtone measurement.

Many familiar chords are explainable as not too far removed members of the overtone series. On the keyboard of a piano the chords are approximations, as the equal temperament necessary in tuning keyboard instruments only gives the suggestion of the chord as it is in the overtones, which are the best basis of measurement. The major triad is produced from the fourth, fifth, and sixth partials; the diminished triad from the fifth, sixth, and seventh partials; different versions of the augmented triad are found by combining the seventh, ninth, and eleventh partials, the eighth, tenth, and thirteenth partials, or the ninth, eleventh, and fourteenth partials. Many different seventh and ninth chords can be found by similar search. The minor triad can be found by combining the sixth, seventh, and ninth partials, or more perfectly by combining the tenth, twelfth, and fifteenth partials.

A very interesting approach to the theoretical explanation of minor is a consideration of the theory of undertones. Until recently undertones were a theory only. Their existence was contested by scientists on the ground that a string or vibrating body could not vibrate at a length greater than its complete length, which gives the fundamental tone. Hence, it was contended, no deeper tones in such a series would be possible of formation on the string. Now, however, Professor

Nicolas A. Garbusov, of the Moscow State Institute for Musicology, has built an instrument on which at least the first nine undertones are easily heard without the aid of resonators. The principle is not that the original sounding body produces the undertones, but that it is difficult to avoid them in resonation. In nearly all musical instruments the tone of the original sounding body is resonated. In a violin, for example, the string is the original sounding body, but the characteristic sound of the violin is produced by the string tones being resonated by the wooden sound-chamber. Professor Garbusov shows that such resonating chambers, under certain circumstances, respond only to every other vibration of the original sounding body, or that some part of the resonator will respond only to every other vibration, even if part of the resonator responds normally to every vibration. The part of the resonator which responds only to every other vibration is then vibrating at one-half the speed of the fundamental and produces a tone one octave lower. Under other circumstances a part of the resonator will vibrate at one-third the speed of the fundamental, thus producing a tone one octave and a fifth below that of the original sounding body. Through an extention of this principle, a series of tones is formed downwards from the fundamental which contains the same relative intervals as the overtone series, counting downwards instead of upwards, and which produces a different actual set of tones. Although such underpartials are

❀❀❀❀❀❀❀❀❀❀❀❀❀❀❀❀❀❀❀❀❀❀❀❀❀❀❀❀❀❀

not apparently produced by the original sounding body, Garbusov shows that, under ordinary conditions of hearing sound in a room, undertones are often added to the original sound by the time it reaches the ear, through the partial resonation of the instrument itself or of objects in the room. The fact that such under-partials are often audible in music makes them of importance in the understanding of certain musical relationships; for just as the second overtone explains the dominant relationship in music, the second undertone explains the subdominant, always a necessary foil to the dominant; and just as the first four overtones form a major triad, the first four undertones form a minor triad, the necessary contrast to the major. Chords formed from the undertones are generated downwards; therefore their roots are really the top notes!

The following chart shows the series of undertones down to the sixteenth underpartial.

The first column gives the serial numbers by which underpartials may be designated. Each fraction indicates what portion of the vibrations per second of the fundamental—in this instance 256—will produce a given undertone. It will be remembered that in the overtone series in order to produce successive overtones the fundamental was multiplied by 2, 3, 4, etc. In the undertone series, on the other hand, the fundamental is divided by 2, 3, 4, etc., to produce successive undertones. The second column, read downwards, gives the notes of the undertone series; notes in parentheses do

Undertone Series Illustrated by Middle C as Fundamental

Serial Nos. of Under-partials (Read down)	Under-tones	Intervals	Vibrations * per Second
	(Fundamental C, generating undertones)		256
1/2	C	Perfect 6th	128 (1/2 of 256)
1/3	F	Perfect 5th	85. 333 (1/3 of 256)
1/4	C	Perfect 4th	64 (1/4 of 256)
1/5	Ab	Major 3rd	51. 2 (1/5 of 256)
1/6	F	Large minor 3rd	42. 667 (1/6 of 256)
1/7	(D)	Small minor 3rd	36. 5714 (1/7 of 256)
1/8	C	Major 2nd	32 (1/8 of 256)
1/9	Bb	Large major second	28. 444 (1/9 of 256)
1/10	Ab	Small major second	25. 6 (1/10 of 256)
1/11	(Gb)	Second	23. 2999 (1/11 of 256)
1/12	F	"	21. 333 (1/12 of 256)
1/13	(Eb)	"	19. 6923 (1/13 of 256)
1/14	(D)	"	18. 2857 (1/14 of 256)
1/15	Db	Large minor second	17. 0667 (1/15 of 256)
1/16	C	Small minor second	16 (1/16 of 256)

* Philosophic pitch.

not coincide in pitch with our present scale system. The third column shows the intervals created between successive undertones; and the fourth column gives the number of vibrations per second of each specific undertone, and its relation to the vibrations of the fundamental.

2. *Polyharmony*

Future progress in enriching harmonic material need not necessarily, of course, follow the one direction thus

✿ ✿

far indicated, ever upwards in the series of overtones. In such a series one fundamental tone is always taken as a base, and it is convenient to take C as a typical example. Now, it is an acoustic fact that overtones can be traced not only from a fundamental tone as a base, but from the overtones themselves as well. Thus the overtone that makes, with the fundamental C, the interval of a fifth is G. From this tone a new and separate series of overtones branches out, and from the overtone E another, and so on. If, then, a simple chord formed on C be played simultaneously with one formed on G and another on E, the resulting complex follows strictly the mathematical principle of overtones. (See Example 1.) Each smaller group of tones derives its

EXAMPLE I

unity from the characteristic quality of its fundamental tone, and the total unity of the group, which might be called a polychord, is derived from the original fundamental tone.

The use of polyharmony, a succession of polychords, is of value as a simplification; for if single harmonies are continually built up by using more and more tones, they become unduly complex; but if these many tones are simplified by a grouping within the harmony into related units, it becomes possible to retain almost complete simplicity and clarity in the use of many different tones together.

Some such simplification may be a necessity. The "neo-classical" movement had its inception in a reaction against over-complexity; but neo-classicists failed to see that the real necessity is to clarify the materials belonging to this age, not to attempt to return to the use of materials which not only have no specific relation to the present time, but were more perfectly handled by classical masters than is possible today. No renaissance in art has ever been entirely successful.

Polyharmony is used by many composers, usually mixed with other types of harmonies rather heterogeneously. It is difficult to find entire passages which flow polyharmonically, and in which the inner chords making up the polychords move logically to harmonies to which they would naturally proceed if the line was of harmony alone. When this is done, polyharmony assumes recognizable shape and can be heard by the ear to have definite meaning. Chords within the polychords have the same relationship as though they were played consecutively; for example, the primary relationship is of chords whose roots are a fifth apart. Thus the polychord built on triads of C, G, and F played simultaneously is the simplest sort of polychord. Following the building of polychords on tones a fifth apart, they may be built on tones a third apart, then on tones a second apart. Polychords may also be formed from different overtones in the same series, of course. This gives a wide gamut of material, and also shows the interrelationships between the chords used, from the simplest to the most complex, an understanding of these relationships being simplified by the application of acoustical law. Such a system still remains to be investigated. In applying this system, the chords within the polychord should be spaced well apart, so that they will not overlap and become confused with each other; as when they are interwoven the effect is not of a polychord, but of a complicated single dissonance. When placed a reasonable distance apart they sound not as elaborate harmonies, but as simple polyharmonies.

If undertones as well as overtones are hypothetically taken as a working basis, the richness of polyharmonic material that can be formed by the combination of relationships with inexorable logic is surprising, for the reason that every tone may be made the base of both major and minor triads. Thus, on the overtones of C we can base the major triad of C, and on the undertones we can base a minor chord, called by its lowest tone, F minor. The nomenclature obscures the fact that the tones of the chord run down the undertone series, with C as its fundamental; but since musicians

are accustomed to name a chord from its lowest tone,
it will be convenient to designate minor chords by their
familiar names.

We can make a simple beginning in mapping out
polyharmonic material by taking C as a base, and placing beside it (1) the simplest related overtone, G, making a fifth above, and (2) the simplest related undertone, F, making a fifth below. The first combinations
to be made are all of the combinations of major chords
that can be based on these three tones. They are found
to be four in number—namely, C major and G major;
C major and F major; G major and F major; and C
major, G major, and F major. The combination of
minor chords possible from the undertones of these related tones are also four in number—namely, F minor
and B flat minor; G minor and F minor; C minor and
B flat minor; and C minor, F minor, and B flat minor.
If now we combine major chords with minor chords
based on these same tones, confining ourselves, for the
sake of simplicity, to combinations of two members,
we find in addition nine possible combinations, as follows: C major and F minor; C major and C minor;
C major and B flat minor; F minor and G major; F
minor and F major; G major and C minor; G major
and B flat minor; C minor and F major; F major and
B flat minor. All these combinations of two members
might be appropriately referred to as polyintervals.
These combinations are merely a beginning of the almost infinite number of groups that might be made out

of the accessible material. They are specifically designated merely to show the method that might be used
in extending indefinitely the list in systematic form.
If we should combine major, minor, augmented, and
diminished chords in groups of three instead of two,
we should add substantially to the list; and from that
point there are two obvious ways of extending the
variety. One is to add to the tones upon which chords
can be based, taking them from the more distant tones
of either the overtone or the undertone series; from
these as starting-points a large number of simple chords,
both major and minor, can be formed. The other way
is to base on this extended system of tones not merely
the simplest chords, but more complex ones, using
material that goes higher in the series of overtones,
and lower in the series of undertones, from any given
tone as a base. By the combination of both methods,
extending both the range of basic chords and the complexity of chords based upon that extended range, a
very great variety of polyharmonic material may be
built up. In order to preserve the distinction between
polyharmony and harmony, it is often advisable to
base the chords of a polyharmony on units which are
more distantly related, so that the resulting complex of
tones does not form or suggest any known single complicated harmony and must, therefore, be analysed by
the ear as being formed of a combination of simpler
chords.

One more consideration of a practical nature remains

to be noted. The units of polyharmony that we have been assuming are simple chords, based on the overtone and undertone series. But as in the practice of harmony we can make use of passing tones—or tones passing along the scale from one chord to another and not necessarily occurring in either—and auxiliary tones —or tones passing along the scale but one note and then returning to the note from which they start— without changing the essential quality of chords as harmonic units, so in polyharmony we can enrich our material by the same methods with equally legitimate effect. This process is called embellishment and is essentially a device of counterpoint. If we use the terms "plain" and "embellished" to distinguish the two ways of treating a given harmonic unit, we can designate three methods of making practical combinations. We can combine polyharmonic material, all the units of which are plain; or we can combine material all the units of which are embellished; or we can make combinations that are mixed, part plain and part embellished. (See Example 2.)

EXAMPLE 2

By a similar use of chords instead of single tones as units, a system of counterpoint of chords may be built up; for instance, a figure of second species counterpoint will be made if in one part a chord remains unchanged, while in another part there is a change of chords. Both changed chords should be related to the unchanged chord, and this relationship can be accomplished by relating the fundamental tones of each of the changed chords with the fundamental of the unchanged chord in correct counterpoint. By following this principle a complete system of counterpoint of

(Single tones on which Polychords are based)

EXAMPLE 3

chords may be formulated. As in polyharmony, the units of such counterpoint may be either plain, embellished, or mixed. (See Example 3.) An appropriate name for counterpoint of chords might be counter-chord, or chord against chord.

Polytonality, or the use of different keys at the same time, may be built up logically by following the same process as in polyharmony. Polytonality is now used in much music, but there is little evidence that polytonal relationships based on acoustics have been taken into consideration.

3. *Tone-quality*

Science has shown that the only possible difference in tone-quality between tones having the same fundamental is through a different relation of dynamics in the overtone series; thus in the tone of a flute even numbered partials are prominent and odd numbered partials are faint, while on the clarinet the reverse is the case. The consequence is that the difference in tone-quality between these instruments is so great that tones which are really the same on them may sound as though they were an octave apart. The result of playing a flute and a clarinet at the same time is an almost perfect series of overtones, and therefore a rich quality of tone.

Science also shows that if the lower partials are more

in evidence in a tone, the result will be a comparatively clear or "pure" tone; if the middle partials, such as those from the third to the ninth or eleventh are more prominent, a thicker or "rich" tone is produced. If very high overtones predominate in a tone, the quality sounds dissonant or discordant in proportion, sometimes even suggesting to the ear that the tone is out of tune.

We find that public taste in the matter of tone-quality has gone in the same direction as in harmony; for formerly, at a time when chords formed from low overtones were considered to be the only concords, the taste was to admire pure tone-quality, which is now seen to be related to such concords by being formed from the same overtones. In the period immediately preceding ours the public taste was for seventh and ninth chords, and a rich tone-quality; the rich quality is formed by a predominance of the same overtones as produce the seventh and ninth chords. Among the contemporary composers who use higher reaches of the overtone series for their harmonic basis, there is a tendency to use more and more dissonant tone-qualities in orchestration. Schönberg, Stravinsky, and many others employ in their scores the upper and lower extreme reaches of orchestral instruments, as well as different sorts of mutes tending to throw the quality of sound into a range in which higher overtones are dominating; sometimes to such an extent that a single tone

33

may sound almost like a dissonance. The overtones prominent in such qualities are the same ones on which the harmonies of these composers are founded.

It will be seen that the problem of forming a related series of tone-qualities is the same as in other branches. A scale can be made by placing in the same group the tone-qualities in which overtones from the same portion of the series are most prominent; thus a quality in which the first overtone is most evident might be number one in the scale; a quality in which the second overtone is most plainly heard might be number two, etc. A quality strongly possessing both the first and the second overtones would be a bridge from number one to number two in the scale, and might be classified as a "harmonic" quality, as it would be produced through a combination of sounds. The harmonic tone-qualities could be named by the chord names of the combinations of overtones forming them; thus, a quality produced by prominence of the fifth, sixth, and seventh partials might be called a "diminished triad tone-quality," because these partials are found to produce a diminished triad, etc.

If tone-qualities were arranged in order, and a notation found for them, it would be of assistance to composer and performer alike. In most ancient music the emphasis was laid on the melody and counterpoint; almost any tone-quality serves to bring out these elements, if well balanced. Since early times, however, more and more music has been and is being written in which certain particular qualities are essential; music which becomes almost completely lost if the wrong quality is given in its production. Tone-quality thus becomes one of the elements in the composition itself and ceases to be only a matter of performance. Since there is no notation of tone-quality, a tradition has grown as to how the tone should be played in Chopin, Debussy, and others; but tradition is a vague thing and is subject to subtle alterations. Chopin and Debussy might be better performed if they had been able to write down the exact shades of tonal values they desired in their works. Progress in the field of new or graduated tone-qualities in composition has been greatly hindered by lack of notation, as it has been justly felt that if music demanding new tonal values were set down in present notation, the desired effect would be likely to be entirely lost in the performance.

4. *Dissonant Counterpoint*

All that has been said relative to the history of music has been considered exclusively from a single point of view—that of tones combined vertically, in musical chords. As a matter of fact, however, this harmonic conception of music has arisen comparatively recently in musical history. The simultaneous combination of different tones came about incidentally to the combining of two or more horizontal series of tones, or melodies, in the practice of counterpoint. As counterpoint

35

became more complex, the resulting simultaneous combinations became more complex, and the problems of harmony arose and were solved.

Turning now to the history of counterpoint as a distinct musical development, we can say that at every stage of increasing complexity of counterpoint, the rules governing choice of intervals grew out of the currently accepted, although sometimes unconscious, harmonic principles of the time. The rules were successively modified, therefore, with the developing progress of harmonic conceptions in successive epochs. Thus the so-called "free" counterpoint taught today differs from "strict" counterpoint, as strict counterpoint differs from still earlier practice.

If we consider the actual practice of Bach in the matter of counterpoint, we find that he made a distinct contribution to the history of counterpoint by using material which suggested harmony of a complexity not accepted before his time; and in doing so he modified the rules of counterpoint so as to assimilate these complexities into a consistent and logical system. As was natural, the fact that he brought innovations into the practice of counterpoint carried his work beyond the comprehension of his contemporaries, who failed to accept fully what he wrote, and took his organ-playing more seriously than his composition. It was only after a hundred years that Mendelssohn's admiration caused Bach's work to be seriously studied as a significant contribution to the development of counterpoint.

❋❋❋❋❋❋❋❋❋❋❋❋❋❋❋❋❋❋❋❋❋❋❋❋❋❋❋❋❋❋❋❋❋❋

The quality in Bach's work that offended his contemporaries was undoubtedly the large infusion of dissonance into his composition. If one considers each harmonic combination formed by his counterpoint, including each passing and auxiliary tone as harmonic elements, the proportion of dissonant chords, varying in different works, is generally large; rising in some works, in fact, to about one-half. Such a proportion might easily suggest the question whether the rules for his practice can really be said to be based on a system of consonant harmony. Study of Bach's principles, of course, shows that his use of dissonance is always subject to certain conditions, and that these conditions by their very nature establish consonant harmony as the basis of his counterpoint. The most significant of these conditions is that dissonance is felt to rely on consonance for resolution.

Turning back now to the history of counterpoint, we notice a curious fact. It was counterpoint, as we have seen, that gave rise originally to the problems of harmony. From the time that harmony was recognized as an independent element in music, counterpoint and harmony went on developing side by side through successive periods; and in both the progress was always one towards complexity, a reaching out to incorporate in the range of musical material ever higher members of the series of overtones. But the striking fact that remains to be noted is that whereas progress in complexity has been in harmony uninterrupted, in counterpoint, practically all such development ceased with the completion of Bach's own work. The rules that arose from a study of his practice have remained stationary until the present time. In apparent contradiction to this statement is the fact that certain fairly recent composers, such as Reger and Franck, introduced into their contrapuntal work passages of dissonant effect distinctly more radical than those of Bach. But closer observation makes it clear that these composers combined with their counterpoint harmonic material of markedly dissonant quality. That which can be analysed as purely contrapuntal is found to follow largely the rules formulated and practised by Bach.

Perhaps the reason for this arrest in development is that Bach's practice was so poised between consonance as a basis and what was felt to be dissonance that it seemed as though any further progress in the one inevitable direction would result in an actual shifting, away from the base of consonant harmony, on to that of frank dissonance; and from the boldness of such a step musicians instinctively held back.

Let us, however, meet the question of what would result if we were frankly to shift the centre of musical gravity from consonance, on the edge of which it has long been poised, to seeming dissonance, on the edge of which it now rests. The difference might not be, any more than in Bach's practice, a matter of numerical proportion between consonant and dissonant effects, but rather an essential dissonant basis, the consonance being felt to rely on dissonance for resolution. An examination in fact would reveal that all the rules of Bach would seem to have been reversed, not with the result of substituting chaos, but with that of substituting a new order. The first and last chords would be now not consonant, but dissonant; and although consonant chords were admitted, it would be found that conditions were in turn applied to them, on the basis of the essential legitimacy of dissonances as independent intervals. In this system major sevenths and minor seconds and ninths would be the foundation intervals; major seconds and ninths, diminished fifths, and minor sevenths might be used as alternatives; all thirds, fourths, fifths, and sixths would only be permitted as passing or auxiliary notes. Octaves would be so far removed from the fundamental intervals in such a system that they would probably sound inconsistent and might not be used except in the rarest circumstances.

The statement about the reversing of rules might seem to imply that the result is a revolution in contrapuntal practice; but it is perhaps more just to consider the change as a gradual one of degree, rather than a radical one of kind, and this for two reasons. First, the development of harmony has since the time of Bach gone so far in the direction of dissonance that effects that were in his time regarded as dissonant tend to be now accepted as essentially consonant. Second, Bach as well as even earlier composers, in their rules, tended to reject the more obvious consonant intervals, such as open octaves, fifths, and fourths; and so in effect cut away the simpler consonant material behind them at the same time that they were employing the more dissonant material that lay before. Therefore if some contemporary composers are found to disfavour the use of thirds and sixths as banal, they are not proving themselves radicals who wish to throw over all that has previously been considered music, but are following the same principle employed in early contrapuntal days—that of prohibiting the use of open fifths, fourths, and octaves, because in a still earlier time these intervals had been overused.

These early contrapuntists did not, of course, entirely reject fifths and fourths from their music; a fifth might, and in fact must, appear as an outer member of the major triad, but the presence of the third lying between was considered to remove the too open effect of the fifth alone. Similarly, the fourth appeared as part of the first or second inversion of the triad. In the same way in dissonant counterpoint all simpler consonant intervals would be permitted, if accompanied at the same time with a seventh, second, or ninth; thus thirds and sixths would not be cut out of music, but would merely have additional intervals added to them.

Some of the music of Schönberg, Ruggles, Hindemith, and Webern seems to denote that they are working out some such procedure as that mentioned above. There is nothing, however, except occasional very good application in their music of the rules that would result from such a counterpoint, to indicate that they use the system consciously, as they have not made public any exposition of their counterpoint. Schönberg, though, has another quite different new system of counterpoint of his own which he has worked out with consistency, which he employs with straightforward logic in his later works, and which is formulated so that he teaches the method to his students.

It may be observed that changing the foundation intervals to be used in counterpoint is a matter of applying contemporary harmonic principles, rather than of adding to the purely contrapuntal possibilities. Schönberg in his system does not formulate new polyphonic materials, but takes from ancient counterpoint devices which had become almost obsolete, such as retrograde, inverse melodic line, etc., as well as better-known contrapuntal usages, and applies them to a twelve-tone scale in which each tone is independent. By an ingenious method of geometric diagram he is able to discover every possible variation of the themes and is therefore able to select the form of development which seems to him the most perfect.

Carl Ruggles has developed a process for himself in writing melodies for polyphonic purposes which embodies a new principle and is more purely contrapuntal than a consideration of harmonic intervals. He finds that if the same note is repeated in a melody before enough notes have intervened to remove the impression of the original note, there is a sense of tautology, because the melody should have proceeded to a fresh note instead of to a note already in the consciousness of the listener. Therefore Ruggles writes at least seven or eight different notes in a melody before allowing himself to repeat the same note, even in the octave.

Whether any of these processes will result in a system eventually accepted can hardly be predicted at the present time; nevertheless, it is interesting to observe that polyphonic progress is being resumed, after resting almost entirely since the time of Bach.

PART II

Rhythm

❀❀❀❀❀❀❀❀❀

Rhythm is a term which has been used in many different ways, and to which different meanings are imparted. To some, rhythm in music means an underlying regular pulse which can be perceived by the hearer; if the music does not contain this pulse, or if the pulse is irregular, it would be called unrhythmic by them. To some, rhythm has to do with accent; to others, with the length of tones.

In this chapter rhythm will be used as a general term, covering all instances of musical phenomena undefinable as sound; sound and rhythm being considered as the two primary elements of music. Subdivisions of rhythm will be considered to be time, or duration of tones; metre, or stress, which has to do with the accenting of tones; and tempo, which has to do with the rate of speed at which tones move. In each instance it will be seen that rhythm is the moving impulse behind the tone, rather than a tangible thing having physical existence. A sound is always necessary to make the rhythm manifest; the concrete expression of any element of rhythm must be through sound. Even when a single tone is sounded, it must have a certain duration, a certain degree of stress must be applied to it, and the rate of speed at which it moves

45

will partly determine its duration; so that all the elements of rhythm are in some degree present in its performance. Nor can it be assumed that a complicated relationship is unrhythmical; if a group of nine notes is played against a group of eleven, the result may sound chaotic to a listener unfamiliar with such a procedure; but to musicians accustomed to cross-rhythms, or to certain peoples who use more complex rhythms, the combination is not only intelligible, but possibly moving. Rhythm presents many interesting problems, few of which have been clearly formulated. Here, however, only one general idea will be dealt with—namely, that of the relationship of rhythm to sound-vibration, and, through this relationship and the application of overtone ratios, the building of ordered systems of harmony and counterpoint in rhythm, which have an exact relationship to tonal harmony and counterpoint.

In the discussion of musical rhythm in its elements, time, metre, and tempo, it will be seen that the problems here considered are not only related to, but based on, principles that are already familiar in the field of harmony and counterpoint—that is, in the relation of tones to one another. In order to make clear the justification in this procedure it will be useful at this point to revert again to what has already been said about the partial series, and by analysis to bring out certain salient facts. The matter may be put graphically as follows:

46

Partial Series	Intervals	Tones	Relative Period of Vibration Time
5	Third	E	| 16 | 16 | 16 | 16 | 16 | = 80
4	Fourth	C	| 16 | 16 | 16 | 16 | = 64
3	Fifth	G	| 16 | 16 | 16 | = 48
2	Octave	C	| 16 | 16 | = 32
1	Fundamental	C	| 16 | = 16

Examining the column at the right, we find that the lines represent graphically the time of one second, in which period the vibrations of the fundamental tone number 16, those of the octave 32, those of the fifth 48, and so on. In other words, in the same time that the fundamental tone gives sixteen vibrations, the second member of the series gives twice sixteen, the third three times sixteen, etc. If we now eliminate the two lower C's, we find that the tones of the simple chord G, C, and E vibrate at the rate of 48, 64, and 80 in the same interval of time. That is, in the time that G is vibrating three, C is vibrating four, and E is vibrating five times. The result, as is graphically shown, is that whereas at no instant within the second of time do the vibrations coincide, at the end of that period all the vibrations coincide. The vibration lengths may thus be thought of as making a sort of pattern, in which the units start at the same instant, separate, and reassemble at a point a fixed distance away; and this they continue to do as long as the tones are sounded together. The reason why the simultaneous tones result in harmony

47

instead of a chaos of sounds is that at regular intervals the vibrations coincide; and in tones forming a musical interval, the smaller the number of units that must be passed over before that coincidence is re-established, the more consonant is the interval. The higher one goes in the overtone series, the greater the number of units that must be passed over, and the further is the effect from one of simple consonance.

If we anticipate for a moment what is to be said in regard to musical rhythm, and desire to represent graphically the result of playing simultaneously three parts which would equally divide a whole note into three, four, and five parts respectively, we should have a diagram of exactly similar form. In this case the larger unit is the measure, the equivalent of one whole note. The smaller units are the fractional notes that perfectly fill the measure. And the principle of beats that coincide, then separate, then coincide again, can be seen to be identical. (See Example 4.)

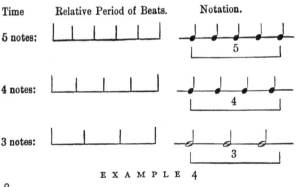

EXAMPLE 4

❋❋❋❋❋❋❋❋❋❋❋❋❋❋❋❋❋❋❋❋❋❋❋❋❋❋❋❋❋❋❋❋❋

With this introduction we may go on to take up in order three elements that go to make up musical rhythm—time, metre, and tempo.

1. *Time*

The accepted fundamental unit with which to measure musical time (or duration) is a whole note. Melody, harmony, and counterpoint might conceivably be made up without departing from this simple time-unit. In practice, of course, variety is introduced, and this by well-known methods. One step is to vary the length of the time-unit by subdividing it into half, quarter, eighth, sixteenth notes, etc. The other step is to combine these longer and shorter units into so-called "figures," which, recurring in a given composition, give it a certain distinctive rhythmical quality.

However great a variety in time effect is made possible by this existing system, certain limitations at once suggest themselves. We are always at liberty to divide a whole note into two halves, a half-note into two quarters, a quarter into two eighth-notes, and so on. And any combination of these lesser time-units is acceptable so long as their sum is the equivalent of the single whole note that we have taken as our base. Rests, subdivided on the same principle as notes, are treated in the same way as their rhythmic equivalents in sounded notes. But if we wish to introduce into a composition a whole measure of normal length

49

divided into three notes of equal length, there is no way of doing so except by the clumsy expedient of writing the figure 3 over three successive half-notes filling a measure. In other words the notes as written down have a certain time-value impossible under the circumstances, and the discrepancy is reconciled by explaining that in reality notes of a different time-value are intended. Were the use of such notes of rare occurrence, this method might be justifiable; since, however, these notes and others having a similar discrepancy in time are very often used, should not an independent method of notation be found for them?

That question may stand for a moment, however, while the subject of time in music is approached from another angle. Assume that we have two melodies moving parallel to each other, the first written in whole notes, and the second in half-notes. If the time for each note were to be indicated by the tapping of a stick, the taps for the second melody would recur with double the rapidity of those for the first. If now the taps were to be increased greatly in rapidity without changing the relative speed, it will be seen that when the taps for the first melody reach sixteen to the second, those for the second melody will be thirty-two to the second. In other words, the vibrations from the taps of one melody will give the musical tone C, while those of the other will give the tone C one octave higher. Time has been translated, as it were, into musical tone. Or, as has been shown above, a parallel can be drawn between the ratio of rhythmical beats and the ratio of musical tones by virtue of the common mathematical basis of both musical time and musical tone. The two times, in this view, might be said to be "in harmony," the simplest possible.

There is a well-known acoustical instrument which produces a sound broken by silences. When the silences between the sound occur not too rapidly, the result is a rhythm. When the breaks between the sound are speeded, however, they produce a new pitch in themselves, which is regulated by the rapidity of the successive silences between the sounds.

There is, of course, nothing radical in what is thus far suggested. It is only the interpretation that is new; but when we extend this principle more widely we begin to open up new fields of rhythmical expression in music.

Referring back to our chart, we find that the familiar interval of a fifth represents a vibration ratio of 2: 3. Translating this into time, we might have a measure of three equal notes set over another in two. A slight complication is now added. Corresponding to the tone interval of a major third would be a time-ratio of five against four notes; the minor third would be represented by a ratio of six against five notes, and so on. If we were to combine melodies in two (or four) beats, three beats, and five beats to the measure, we should then have three parallel time-systems corresponding to the vibration speeds of a simple consonant harmony.

EXAMPLE 5

(See Example 5.) The conductor of such a trio, by giving one beat to a measure, could lead all the voices together; for the measure, no matter what time divisions it included, would begin and end at the same instant.

Into the fundamental variety of such a system incidental variety could be introduced in two ways. First,

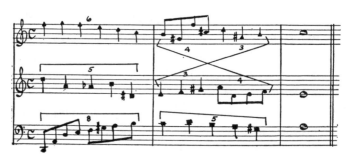

EXAMPLE 6

❀❀❀❀❀❀❀❀❀❀❀❀❀❀❀❀❀❀❀❀❀❀❀❀❀❀❀❀❀❀❀❀

the result of all this could be a single continuous rhythmic harmony in which the units of the time-scheme
could shift from one voice to another. (See Example
6.) Or, as would usually be the case, if greater variety
were desired, the complete rhythmic harmony could
be changed at will, so that the effect would correspond
to a succession of different chords, in the selection of
which the principles of tonal harmony might be observed. (See Example 7.)

E X A M P L E   7

The second method of securing variety would be to
divide and subdivide the notes of any given time-value,
just as in present-day music whole notes are divided
into halves, quarters, etc. Obviously, if the measure is
to be divided on the principle of three beats, the note

that would take up one-half of the measure would be one and a half beats long. The measure would be completed, then, in another half-beat and a whole. A convenient mathematical representation would be: $\frac{3}{6} + \frac{1}{6} + \frac{2}{6} = \frac{6}{6} = 1$. The half-beat required in subdividing measures of an uneven number of beats (five, seven, etc.) is nothing but another application of the principle of the dotted note: $\frac{2}{8} + \frac{3}{8} + \frac{1}{8} + \frac{2}{8} = \frac{8}{8} = 1$.

In order to speak accurately of notes of new time-values, they might be given distinctive names. At present a note occupying one-fourth the time of a whole note is called a quarter-note. Consequently, instead of calling a note occupying a third the time of a whole note a "half-note triplet," why not refer to it as a third-note? Hereafter in this work a note will be designated by a fractional number indicating what portion of a whole note it occupies.

It would be found in practice that in order to establish certain ratios groups might have to be used which include fractions; for example, if the lower octave of a note the ratio of which is eleven were to be used, the proper ratio would be five and one-half notes in a single measure. The kind of notes used to express such a ratio would be the equivalent of two eleventh-notes tied together, and might be termed two-elevenths notes. By accepting the smallest fraction as one count, the proportionate time of any fractional or other notes can be counted easily. Thus, in the previous example five two-elevenths notes and one eleventh-note would

54

✤ ✤

be used in a measure, and if one count were given to the eleventh-note, and two counts each to the two-elevenths notes, a total of eleven counts would be obtained for the measure as a whole.

It will be seen that while there has been some use of such time-values as eleven in the time of a whole note, the conception of a two-elevenths note is new; and by treating other rhythmic ratios in the same way, many other time-values are obtained which are unfamiliar in music; also by dotting a two-elevenths note, a three-elevenths note is obtained; by doubling it, a four-elevenths note, etc. These finer rhythmical distinctions open up a new field for investigation. Not only do nearly all Oriental and primitive peoples use such shades of rhythm, but also our own virtuosi, who, instead of playing the notes just as written, often add subtle deviations of their own.

Professor Hornbusel, of Berlin, has made the experiment of recording the time-values of a passage, as actually played by a capable musician, notated as in Example 8. He found that the lengths of notes as

E X A M P L E 8

played were quite irregular; for example, the first of the first two eighth-notes was almost twice as short as the second, while the quarter-note following was not twice as long as either of the eighth-notes.

55

Our system of notation is incapable of representing any except the most primary divisions of the whole note. It becomes evident that if we are to have rhythmical progress, or even cope with some rhythms already in use, and particularly if we are to continue with our scheme of related rhythms and harmonies, new ways of writing must be devised to indicate instantly the actual time-value of each note. We are dealing, of course, not with three-fourths metre, five-fourths metre, etc., but with a whole note divided into three or five equal parts.

There is readily suggested, however, a modification of the notation system based upon familiar musical practice. In our present notation the shape of notes is the same; their time-value, whether whole notes, half-notes, quarter-notes, etc., is designated by printing the note as open or solid and by adding stems and hooks. All that need be done, then, is to provide new shapes for notes of a different time-value—triangular, diamond-shaped, etc. The use of open and solid notes, of stems, and of hooks is equally applicable to these notes of varied shape. A few adjustments in regard to designating rests would make the system complete.

The shapes of the new notes are necessarily arbitrary, except in the use of triangular notes for the third-note series, since a shape suggestive of the number of a series would be too complicated for practical purposes. Notes of new shape are provided for the new series up to the ninth-note series. For the basic

56

note of all new series above a tenth-note in value, a stroke drawn diagonally downwards from left to right through the basic note of an earlier series indicates that the number ten has been added to its original value. This obviates the necessity of inventing new shapes for notes of higher series. For instance, a stroke through any note of the whole-note series indicates that ten has been added to the number one represented by a whole note, and that the note in question belongs to the eleventh-note series. For the thirteenth-note series a stroke will be drawn through a note of the third-note series, etc. As is at present the practice in the series now in use, that of whole notes, the divisions to obtain fractional notes in the proposed new series will be by two; and since the bases of these new series are themselves fractional notes, notes less than a whole note in value, obtained by multiplying any basic note by two, are included in the series to which the basic note belongs. Thus, a third-note multiplied by two gives a two-thirds note, which is not only twice the length of a third-note in value, but will form three equal notes in the time of two whole notes—six third-notes. The following chart (Example 9) shows the shapes chosen for the notes of the new series:

The use of square note-heads is helpful in suggesting the relation between fifteenth-notes and fifth-notes. Fifteenth-notes are the same as triplets in the fifth-note system, and a dotted fifteenth-note is the same as a tenth-note.

The fundamental relationship between rhythmic values in the same system, such as between a third-note and a sixth-note, which have a 1:2 relationship, is seen at once by the similarity of note-heads. Another advantage is that metres formed by the use of odd-note

Whole Note Series.
Oval-shaped notes

Whole note: ○ half note: ♩ quarter note: ♩ 8th note: ♪ 16th note: ♪ 32nd note: ♪

Third Note Series.
Triangular-shaped notes

2-3rds note: △ 3rd note: ♩ 6th note: ♩ 12th note: ♪ 24th note: ♪ 48th note: ♪

Fifth Note Series.
Square notes

4-5ths note: □ 2-5ths note: ▢ 5th note: ♩ 10th note: ♪ 20th note: ♪ 40th note: ♪

Seventh Note Series.
Diamond-shaped notes

4-7ths note: ◇ 2-7ths note: ♢ 7th note: ♩ 14th note: ♪ 28th note: ♪ 56th note: ♪

Ninth Note Series.
Oblong notes

8-9ths note: ▭ 4-9ths note: ▰ 2-9ths note: ▮ 9th note: ▮ 18th note: ▮ 36th note: ♪

Eleventh Note Series.
Oval notes with stroke

8-11ths note: ♮ 4-11ths note: ♮ 2-11ths note: ♮ 11th note: ♪ 22nd note: ♪ 44th note: ♪

Thirteenth Note Series.
Triangular notes with stroke

8-13ths note: ♮ 4-13ths note: ♮ 2-13ths note: ♮ 13th note: ♪ 26th note: ♪ 52nd note: ♪

Fifteenth Note Series.
Square notes with stroke

8-15ths note: ♮ 4-15ths note: ♮ 2-15ths note: ♮ 15th note: ♪ 30th note: ♪ 60th note: ♪

EXAMPLE 9

values, such as ²⁄₆ metre, etc., become possible to notate. Such metre and time relationships are a natural development, but have been inhibited by being unnotatable. The practical meaning of ²⁄₆ metre is that notes of triplet time-value are accented in groups of two instead of in groups of three. Still another possibility

❀❀❀❀❀❀❀❀❀❀❀❀❀❀❀❀❀❀❀❀❀❀❀❀❀❀❀❀❀❀

opened up by the new notation is that of separating
notes of triplet or other time-values by placing between
them notes of other systems. Thus in old notation three
triplet notes or their equivalent must always be used
together; in the new notation perhaps only one triplet note will be used between quarter-notes, as in the
following example: Example 10.

E X A M P L E   1 0

Thus far it has been assumed that time-changes occur only between measures. Should such practice be
actually necessary, a certain inflexibility would result,
just as if a single chord must extend through the
whole of the measure in which it stands. In reality,
however, there is nothing to prevent more than one
time-scheme from being included within a single measure; such a scheme does not have to fall within the
limits of a whole note; all that is necessary is to see
that the fractional divisions of each time-scheme fill
the time allotted to that time-scheme. Thus, let us
say that we wished to use a ratio of 2:3 in one half
of a measure and to use another of 5:4 in the other
half. In the first half, two quarter-notes might be set
over against three sixth-notes; and the first half of the
measure would be evenly filled. Then, if four eighth-
notes and five tenth-notes were used in the second

half, the measure would be accurately completed. (See
Example 11.) The fraction chosen need not be so

EXAMPLE 11

obvious as in this example. Any element in any ratio
can be variously expressed. Thus, the ratio 2:3, reduced to 1:1½, could as well be expressed by one
half-note, against one third-note plus one ninth-note;
and the ratio of 5:4, reduced to 2½:2, by two fifth-
notes plus one tenth-note, against two quarter-notes.
Naturally, much more flexibility would result from this
practice than from making each new ratio continuous
throughout a measure. (See Example 12.)

EXAMPLE 12

A further variety is also possible. That is, one time-
ratio might be continued in one part while a change

is instituted in a corresponding part. When this is done
in tones, the result is one of the figures in strict counterpoint—namely, the second species. In the field of
rhythm the example given is a simple figure of rhythmic counterpoint; and it may be seen that by further
application of this system all the effects of counterpoint
are capable of being expressed in rhythm. (See Example 13.)

Another matter remains to be touched upon: the use
of rhythmic figures, so attractive in familiar music. It

EXAMPLE 13

is evident that figures can be used in rhythmic ratios as in ordinary rhythms. Thus, a rhythmic figure based on a quarter-note results whenever a combination of smaller notes is made, by the use of eighth-notes, dotted eighths and sixteenths, etc., the sum of which equals a quarter-note. If, then, in writing a time-ratio of 3:4 we have already used four figures instead of the four quarter-notes, it is a simple matter, if we so desire, to divide the three third-notes into corresponding figures, by the use of sixth-notes, dotted sixths and twelfths, etc. In either case the accent would come on the first notes of the respective figures, and the sense of the fundamental time-ratio would not be broken, but instead its units would be pleasingly varied. (See Example 14.)

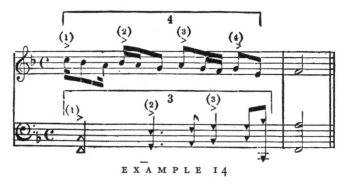

EXAMPLE 14

An interesting series of time-values is to be found by further investigation of the possibilities of the dotted note. The most customary way of using dotted notes is to fill out the value of a dotted note by a shorter note equal in value to the time of the dot itself, the complete time occupied being that of a longer note in the usual rhythmic system. Thus a dotted quarter-note will be followed by an eighth-note, occupying the time of a half-note altogether. If the metre signature is ⁶⁄₈, successions of dotted eighth-notes are familiar. If, however, we make a succession of eighth- or sixteenth-notes in ¼ metre, we arrive at unusual time-values, although certain of the values obtained are to be found occasionally in music. Brahms, for example, often uses four equal notes in a metre of ¾, to fill a measure; these notes may be written as four quarter-notes with a figure four over them, but it is more exact to notate them as four dotted eighth-notes. If we make a series of dotted whole, half-, quarter-, eighth-, and sixteenth-notes, we find that they are related, just as ordinary whole, half-, and quarter-notes are, through each being one-half the value of the next in the series. (See Example 15.) Customary use of dotted notes does not suggest the interesting modes of employment possible

Whole note series.		Dotted note series.	
Whole note:	𝅝	Dotted whole note:	𝅝 .
Half note:	𝅗𝅥	Dotted half note:	𝅗𝅥 .
Quarter note:	♩	Dotted quarter note:	♩ .
Eighth note:	♪	Dotted eighth note:	♪ .
Sixteenth note:	𝅘𝅥𝅯	Dotted sixteenth note:	𝅘𝅥𝅯 .

EXAMPLE 15

by an understanding of their relationship to each other in an independent series.

Double-dotted notes, also familiar in music, can in the same way be formed into a separate series.

Separate systems can be based as well on dotted notes of the irregular series, such as dotted fifth- or seventh-notes. It is noteworthy that dotted notes in the third-note system have the same value as ordinary notes in the familiar whole- and half-note system and are often useful in relating the two systems; dotted ninth-notes become the same as sixth-notes, and therefore fall into the third-note system; dotted fifteenth-notes fall into the fifth-note system.

An argument against the development of more diversified rhythms might be their difficulty of performance. It is true that the average performer finds cross-rhythms hard to play accurately; but how much time does the average performer spend in practising them? Cross-rhythms are difficult and must be familiar before proficiency can be obtained in performing them; but if even a few minutes a day are seriously devoted to mastering them, surprising results are obtained. Surely they are as well worth learning as the scales, which students sometimes practise hours a day for years. By experiment we have observed that such rhythms as five against six against eight or nine, and other combinations of three rhythms together, can be quite accurately performed by the devotion of about fifteen minutes a day for about six months. Some of the rhythms de-

veloped through the present acoustical investigation
could not be played by any living performer; but these
highly engrossing rhythmical complexes could easily
be cut on a player-piano roll. This would give a real
reason for writing music specially for player-piano,
such as music written for it at present does not seem
to have, because almost any of it could be played instead by two good pianists at the keyboard.

(a)

(b)

EXAMPLE 16

It is highly probable that an instrument could be devised which would mechanically produce a rhythmic
ratio, but which would be controlled by hand and
would therefore not be over-mechanical. For example,
suppose we could have a keyboard on which when C
was struck; a rhythm of eight would be sounded; when

65

D was struck, a rhythm of nine; when E was struck, a rhythm of ten. By playing the keys with the fingers, the human element of personal expression might be retained if desired. It is heartily proposed that such an instrument to play the scale of time-values given at the end of this chapter be constructed. On such a keyboard one might make many variations, such as playing a rhythmic chord as an arpeggio, which would result in starting the rhythmical units canonically. (See Example 16.)

2. Metre

The next element of musical rhythm that calls for consideration is metre, the result of rhythmically regular accent. Musical time, as we have seen, assumes a certain unit as a base, and it has been convenient to use the simplest, a single whole note. Variation is effected by the different systems of fractional subdivisions, such as three third-notes, five fifth-notes, etc. Musical metre, on the other hand, assumes a succession of time-units, usually quarter- or eighth-notes, and introduces variety by accenting certain of these notes at fixed intervals. Thus, the distinction between ¾ "time," ¼ "time," ⁵⁄₄ "time," etc., is a matter of musical metre. If desired, new metres could be made by using the new kinds of notes suggested in the time-scheme, ⅔, ⅗, etc. The purely metrical consideration, that of accent, would not be changed by so doing, but such new metres are often invaluable in combining metre and time-ratios.

❋❋❋❋❋❋❋❋❋❋❋❋❋❋❋❋❋❋❋❋❋❋❋❋❋❋❋❋❋❋❋❋

It is here proposed to apply the principle of the series of partials to musical metre, as it has already been applied to musical time. If it be found that certain metrical combinations have a mathematical correspondence to certain tonal combinations, it will be found possible to combine metres by mathematical ratios into metrical harmonies, just as tones are combined into tonal harmonies. In order to avoid the complications of combinations of time and metre, which will be considered later, in the subject of metre alone a standard unit of time will be taken on which all the metres here treated of will be based. This unit, on account of its universal metrical use and the fact that it is a close approach to a mean between a slow and a fast note, will be a quarter-note.

Just as in the matter of tone we start with a simple fundamental tone like the C of sixteen vibrations to the second, so we base our metrical system on a simple base. A measure of ¾ metre, if completed in exactly one second (which would be the case if the metronome were set at 120), bears a direct relation to the tone C of sixteen vibrations, since if this tone were carried down three octaves, the result would be a vibration, or rhythm, of two impulses to the second. Taking, then, ¾ metre as the base, we look for what would correspond metrically to the octave of a fundamental tone. We find it by putting a measure of ¼ metre over against two measures of ¾ metre, thus creating a ratio in which double the number of units are marked by a

single metrical accent, just as the octave has double the
number of vibrations in a given unit of time. Corresponding to the third partial would be a metre related
to the base as three to one; and we have a measure of
6/4 metre, set over against three measures of 2/4 metre.
It is thus a simple matter to build up a table in which
metrical units related to the given fundamental base
correspond to tone values related to a given fundamental tone, as the metrical accents will form similar ratios
between one another. The table that follows shows the
metrical correspondence to the series of partial tones
up to the sixth partial:

Serial No. (Read up.)	Tone	Intervals	Metre on 2/4 Base
6	G	Minor third	12/4 (6/4, 3/4, 6/8)
5	E	Major third	10/4 (10/8, 5/4)
4	C	Fourth	8/4 (4/4, 2/4)
3	G	Fifth	6/4 (6/8, 3/4)
2	C	Octave	4/4 (4/8, 2/2)
1	C	Fundamental	2/4

It will be seen that within the brackets are included
certain metrical equivalents for the metres of the regular series. The reason is simple. It is often convenient
to raise or lower a given tone to a different octave in
order to combine it with other tones in a chord. Thus,
in the table given, C appears three times: in the fundamental, the octave, and the second octave. And G,
whether it appears in the interval of the fifth or the
minor third, is a similar tone. So too in the scale of

✾ ✾

metres: the base ⅔4 may be expressed as ⅘8 or ⁹⁄16, and
for it may be substituted ¼, ⁸⁄4, etc. In the same way
the metrical ratio corresponding to the tone G is similar, whether we express it as ⁶⁄4, ⁶⁄8, ¾, etc. This table,
then, extended as far as may be desired, furnishes a key
to the system that it is proposed to apply. A chromatic
scale of metres will be found at the end of this chapter.

The simplest way of using metrical rhythms on the
analogy of musical tones is to keep shifting the metrical
units in successive measures. If the changes be made,
as is often done in the work of Stravinsky, in all the
parts at the same time, the result is analogous to a simple melody in tone. To some persons, even so slight a
change as this seems unrhythmical and abstruse. This
may be due to a lack of consideration of how extremely
primary the older conception of metre is, in which the
same metre is expected to remain unchanged for an
entire composition. If in lieu of a melody the same note
were to be repeated for an entire work, it would be
considered absurd; yet this endless repetition is just
what is expected in metre, in which hundreds of the
same metrical units, such as measures of ¾, etc., follow
one another without change.

It is perhaps this condition of metrical monotony
which has caused a widespread feeling that the metrical accent is always to be disguised; there is a large
school of musicians who teach that to hear the metrical
accent is always boring, and who construct the phras-
ing across the bar-line in such a fashion as partly to

negate the metre. Beethoven was chafing against the
lack of metrical interest when he introduced the famous sforzandos on weak beats, which are so clear a
mark of his style. Jazz music represents another unconscious reaction against too regular metre, since not
only are its syncopations accented off the main beat,
but the bass is almost always accented on the two weak-
est beats of the ¼ measure—namely, the second and
fourth—while the main beats remain comparatively unaccented. The reaction was so strong in Eric Satie and
some of his followers that they did away with metre
altogether and wrote no bar-lines. This did not mean
that there was no metre in their music, in which the
accents were simply irregular and might have been notated as changing metres. Such a notation would make
their music easier to read, since at present the performer has no means of deciding where these composers wished notes accented, or where to find the underlying pulse which at times undoubtedly exists in their
music.

What is required to re-create interest in metre is not
to do away with so powerful a musical element, nor to
keep the bar-lines always the same and then negate
them by accents; because accents within the measure
are never felt to be the same as first beats in the metre.
Neither is it necessary to make of metre a sort of
skeleton-in-the-closet, as though it were an evil thing,
essential to preserve, but so unlovely that it must be
covered by almost any accenting of phrase which will

✿✿✿✿✿✿✿✿✿✿✿✿✿✿✿✿✿✿✿✿✿✿✿✿✿✿✿✿✿✿✿✿✿

disguise the metrical foundation. All of these devices are interesting in music, but it does not seem amiss to get at the root of the trouble and bring the possibilities of metrical variety up to the same standards now applied to other branches. When metres change frequently, or when harmonies are formed from them, they give pleasure, and it is again of interest to hear them clearly defined, instead of disguised. On first hearing, of course, some listeners may not prove able to differentiate between such rhythms. In this case they may sometimes find abstruse and monotonous metres which really contain more variety than the rhythms which are better understood by them. Ability to perceive fine distinctions of rhythm is perhaps rarer than a similar ability in tone. Composers who innovate new rhythms often pass unnoticed; and their music, particularly if it contains consonant harmonies, may be branded as imitative.

It is possible to make metrical change in one part while another is being made in another part, the two metres having a certain degree of independence; as: $\begin{vmatrix} x & x & x & x & x \\ x & x & x & x & x \end{vmatrix}$ Here we have the germ of two independent melodies running parallel to each other, yet not haphazard; in a word, counterpoint. In order to build up this system of counterpoint it is unnecessary to consider metres as units of ratio. They are not haphazard, because care must be taken to apply to the melodic succession of these metres the general principles relating to their corresponding tones.

In order to emphasize to the ear the relationship between parts, it is well for the accents of both parts to coincide with reasonable frequency, except in instances where the relationship is clearly heard as a canon, in which the accents may never coincide. (See Example 17.)

EXAMPLE 17

The matter becomes somewhat more complicated when we begin to apply the principles of harmony to the use of musical metre. If we wish to strike what we might call a metrical chord, we should first pick out our metres with reference to the given base, and then we should employ these metres simultaneously in different parts. Let us assume a simple interval of two tones, say C and G represented by the metrical ratios ²⁄₄, ³⁄₄. We should have this result $\begin{vmatrix} x\ x|x\ x|x\ x|x\ x|x\ x|x\ x \\ x\ x\ x|x\ x\ x|x\ x\ x|x\ x\ x \end{vmatrix}$. The two metres would begin together, separate, and reunite to begin again together, and so on indefinitely. The vibrations of the corresponding partials, it will be

❀❀❀❀❀❀❀❀❀❀❀❀❀❀❀❀❀❀❀❀❀❀❀❀❀❀❀❀❀❀❀

recalled, go through a precisely analogous cycle. Thus:

$$\left\{ \begin{array}{l} 32 \quad + \quad 32 \quad + \quad 32 = 96 \text{ vibrations} \\ 2 \times 16 + 2 \times 16 + 2 \times 16 \\ \quad 48 \quad + \quad\quad 48 = 96 \text{ vibrations} \\ 3 \times 16 \quad + \quad 3 \times 16 \end{array} \right.$$

We might liken the result to a chain made up of successive links, which join at the points where the accents coincide. And the length of a link, it will be seen, is determined by multiplying the numbers of notes in the respective measures together, in this case two by three. If now we wish to strike a metrical chord of three voices, the same principles are applied, but with considerable addition to the complexity of the result. A characteristic example would be a chord (corresponding to the tonal chord C, G, and E) based on the metres $\frac{2}{4}$, $\frac{3}{4}$, and $\frac{5}{4}$. Obviously, each metre would be separately related to two others. Thus, if we name the metres as given X, Y, and Z, X would form a link with Y every sixth note, but with Z every tenth note. And Y, linking itself with comparative frequency with X, would complete its link with Z only after fifteen notes. These smaller links, finally, would combine into a great link after twice fifteen, or thirty, notes were completed. Within this great link the smaller link X-Y would be five times completed, the link X-Z three times, the Y-Z twice. (See Example 18.) To construct a succession of these great metrical links would be like striking a chord repeatedly at the beginning of successive measures.

73

For regularity such as this there is, of course, no need; as in tonal harmony, there are different ways of bringing variety into the use of musical metre. One way is to change the metrical chord when the large link has been completed—to build the composition, as it were, on a series of different metrical chords. An-

EXAMPLE 18

EXAMPLE 18

other way is to interrupt a given chord before the completion of the great metrical link and to begin a new metrical chord at once. The principle is that when a sufficient number of the smaller links have passed to establish the identity of the metrical chord, a new chord can be struck without causing a sense of confusion to the listener's ear. By this method it is possible

EXAMPLE 19

75

EXAMPLE 19

for metrical harmonies to succeed each other in quicker succession that if it were necessary to carry each great link to its close. (See Example 19.) Another method of producing metrical harmony is to form a harmonic ratio from metrical accents instead of links. In this system the ratio 2: 3: 5 would be produced by placing five measures of $\frac{6}{4}$ over against three measures of $\frac{10}{4}$, over against two measures of $\frac{15}{4}$. (See Example 20.)

Yet another resource of metrical variety grows out of what has been said. It is a commonplace of musical composition that a given grouping of tones made be regarded vertically, as a succession of chords, or horizontally, as a combination of simultaneous melodies; as harmony, that is to say, or as counterpoint. And counterpoint may be simple, consisting, say, of two simultaneous melodies, or it may be more complex, as when a melody is set over against a succession of tones grouped harmonically. A method of adapting metrical combinations to the simpler kind of counterpoint has already been suggested by an easy example. Enough has been said now to show the possibility of joining what might be called metric melody contrapuntally with material metrically harmonic. This may be done by relating the successive metrical units (corresponding to tones) of one part according to the principle of counterpoint, while the units of the simultaneous parts are selected and grouped according to the principle of harmony. (See Example 21.)

Counterpoint of a somewhat more complicated

77

EXAMPLE 20

nature, based on the conception of metres as units of ratio, is another possibility. Thus, we might have four
parts proceeding simultaneously, each with its independent metre, yet harmonically related. The result,
as has been shown, is metrical harmony. But if now we
should continue two of the parts while we changed the

EXAMPLE 21

EXAMPLE 21

ratio of the other two parts, we have a result that might

be represented thus:
$$\left\{\begin{array}{l} l\ldots\ldots\ldots\ldots\ldots\ldots\ldots\ldots \\ m\ldots\ldots\ldots\ldots\ldots\ldots\ldots \\ n\ldots\ldots\ldots\ldots p\ldots\ldots\ldots \\ o\ldots\ldots\ldots\ldots q\ldots\ldots\ldots \end{array}\right. \bullet$$

The relation between the upper and lower parts is now
contrapuntal, and a special method of establishing metrical counterpoint has been laid down. Thus, once the
method of building melodies and harmonies out of
metrical units has been established, all the diversity of
application possible to the treatment of musical tone
becomes possible also in the treatment of musical
metre.

3. *Dynamics*

Musical metre is usually considered to pertain to
regularly recurring accent, and it has been so treated
here. Since, however, the term "metre" covers all exig-
encies of accent in music, the subject of dynamics, or
degrees of stress (or shading, as it is sometimes
termed), will be seen to be related to metre. In the
subject of recurrent metres, it is assumed that there
will be theoretical accents of heavy stress on the first
beat of any measure, light beats in unaccented portions
of the measure, and perhaps medium stress applied to
secondary accents within the measure. This gives only
three different shades of dynamics, while in actual use
there are many subtle differences; performers who have
the ability to control delicate dynamic shades gain

instant appreciation, and probably no other one element in performance produces such sure emotional reactions from the auditor; control of dynamics may often mark the difference between a masterly and a mediocre performer. In spite of its importance, there is no adequate notation for dynamics, and the fine distinctions are left to the performer, although such distinctions might well be considered an essential part of composition. When a performer produces fine dynamics, he is really supplying an element of composition and is creating a rhythmic form into which to pour the tonal mass. Often the performer has wider knowledge of dynamics, or feeling for them, than the composer, since dynamics has been far too little considered by composers as an essential element of composition, perhaps owing to the inadequacy of the notation. We are able to notate only a few shades: *ppp, pp, p, mp, mf, f, ff, fff*; and these are only relative; who can say exactly how soft *p* is, or exactly the loudness of a *ff*?

Science can measure the loudness of sound by a number of well-known means. Since we have a familiar instrument for measuring so delicate a thing as rate of speed—namely, a metronome—it would seem that we should also have some simple instrument for the measurement of stress. Then we could devise scales of degrees of stress, each successive note of which might represent the addition of one shade more or less of stress, a very fine distinction being accepted as a unit. Notation would then include an indication of how many units of stress should be applied to any particular tone. This might be done on an additional staff, if desired. If such units were defined, we should be able to apply the familiar principle of the overtone relationships; thus eight units against nine units would represent a ratio of 8:9, represented also by the relation between the eighth and ninth partials in the overtone series. By following such a system of related ratios, dynamic shadings might become formulated into a well-ordered scale system and become a more definite element of musical composition.

Crescendo and diminuendo in dynamics is the same in many ways as sliding tone in pitch; and undoubtedly a definite relation could be found between a certain curve of changing pitch, and a similar curve in a gradual reducing or increasing of loudness or softness. The points from which such dynamic slides start and the points to which they proceed could be determined by the system of units proposed, and the type of curve or degree of angle taken by the dynamic line could thus be graphically measured and notated. Also the dynamic lines, if several were in process, would be found to have at any point a specific and measurable relationship to each other. Acceleration and retardation in tempo, which belong to the same category as sliding pitch and crescendo and diminuendo, are treated later. All three of these elements have specific relationships to each other, and form a special branch for investigation.

4. *Form*

Just as single tones are grouped together rhythmically to form a measure, successions of measures are grouped rhythmically, in the construction of musical form. The rhythm of mòst classical forms is in twos, fours, eights, etc.; a group of eight measures ending with a half-cadence, or part question, answered by a similar eight measures ending on a full cadence, or definite conclusion, is a familiar method of building; and often a second section will contain a new theme in contrast to the theme in the first section, and the first section will be repeated in some form to close. Since some of the links formed by metrical harmonies are long, it would be interesting to consider such a link as a definite new form into which suitable musical material could be poured. Such a form would make for perfection of outline, and it would give a clarity and purpose to the composition as a whole, which are often lacking in works using experimental material. It would be found that the type of metrical combinations near the centre of the great link would be a contrast to those at the beginning, so that the principle of a contrasting middle section would be suggested; and that the smaller links in the latter half of the great link would be an exact reverse of the first part, so that there would be a recapitulation of the first theme, in reverse, at the close. Other ways of varying metre might be also applied to musical form. It would be interesting to investigate possibilities of irregular sections. Numerous classical composers have written occasional irregular sections, usually with such skill that the average listener is unaware that unusual rhythm has been employed. Much contemporary composition contains irregular sections, or an odd number of measures in a section, but it is not customary to sustain a certain scheme of form throughout a composition. Professor Conus, of the conservatory of Moscow, has developed an ingenious system of making symmetrical form out of irregular numbers of measures. As a whole, however, there has been in contemporary music less development in form than in harmony or melody, and less than in other forms of rhythm. Therefore the creation of new definite forms is a fertile field.

5. Metre and Time Combinations

Although it is not in general the purpose of this work to treat of combinations, a grasp of the subject of the combinations of metre and time seems essential to an understanding of metre alone. In order to treat of metre alone, it was necessary to apply the metres to a constant time-unit, a quarter-note being chosen for this purpose. This fixes a definite length of time and definite metres for the completion of any given metrical ratio. For instance, if the ratio is 2: 3, the time must be two times three, or six, quarter-notes; and the metres must be a metre of two, or 2/4, against a metre of three, or 3/4.

If, instead of taking a quarter-note as a time-unit, we choose notes of other time-values, it becomes possible to express any metrical ratio in any given length of time and in any metre; which not only gives greater flexibility, but also reduces the undue length of time it takes to complete certain ratios in the system of metre alone. It can be seen that in employing this method, not only a metrical relation must be considered, but also, since the simultaneous metres may be built on different time-values, the relation between these various time-values must be taken into account.

When a metre of two is spoken of, it is meant that as a metrical unit an accented note is followed by an unaccented note. Similarly a metre of three means that an accented note is followed by two unaccented notes. The kind of notes on which these accents fall, is not a matter of metre, but of time. When it is desired to form a metrical ratio one of the component numbers of which is two, it does not necessarily follow that a metre of two is to be used. What should be remembered is that a certain length of time must contain two metrical accents, one at the beginning of the time period and one on the first note after half the time period has elapsed. Thus, if we wish to form a metrical ratio of two against three, using quarter-notes as a base, the time period of the ratio will be six quarter-notes. The element of two in the ratio is expressed, not by metres of two, but by two measures of a metre of three, since when the accents have been properly placed, one at the beginning of the

86

time period and the other after it has been half completed—that is, on the first and the fourth notes—it is
found that two unaccented notes follow each accented
note, thus producing a metre of three. The element of
three in the ratio is expressed by a metre of two, since,
when three accents have been equally distributed
through the time period—namely, on the first, third,
and fifth notes—an unaccented note will follow an accented note, thus forming a metre of two.

Suppose, now, that we wish to express the metrical
ratio of two against three in the time of one whole note,
instead of in the time of six quarter-notes; and instead
of having a metre of two in one part and a metre of
three in the other, to have both parts in a metre of two.
On the face of it this seems impossible, as indeed it
would be if we confined ourselves to a base of quarter-
notes. If, however, in the part expressing the element of
two in the ratio we place two measures of ⅔ metre,
and in the part expressing the element of three in the
ratio, three measures of ⅔ metre, we have accomplished our purpose. (See Example 22.) Two-four is a
metre of two since in its use an accented note is followed by an unaccented note; and two measures of ⅔

EXAMPLE 22

metre, dividing as they do the time of a whole note into
two equal accents, correctly express the element of two
in the ratio. Two-six is also a metre of two, since in its
use an accented note is followed by an unaccented
note; and three measures of ⅖, dividing as they do the
time of one whole note into three equal accents, correctly express the element of three in the ratio. Thus
the metrical ratio of two against three has been formed,
and in its formation notes of two different time-values
have been used. In the time of one whole note, four
quarter-notes were used in one metre against six sixth-
notes in the other metre. The time-ratio, then, is seen
to be four against six, which is reducible to two against
three, and is the same as the metrical ratio. This coincidence of the time-ratio and the metre-ratio is accidental and even unusual. Except where there is such
a coincidence, the combinations of metres will produce
one ratio and the combinations of times another. Since
each of these ratios is the equivalent of a different tonal
interval, or chord, the relation between these two ratios
is of necessity polyharmonic. Take, for instance, the
metrical ratio of two against three formed by a metre

EXAMPLE 23

of four against a metre of six, to be completed in the
time of two whole notes. Set two measures of ¼ metre
over against three measures of ⁶⁄₉ metre. (See Example
23.) The ¼ metre is a metre of four since in its use an
accented note is followed by three unaccented notes, and
two measures of ¼, dividing as they do the time of
two whole notes into two equal accents, correctly express the element of two in the ratio. Six-nine is a metre
of six, since in its use an accented note is followed by
five unaccented notes; and three measures of ⁶⁄₉ metre,
dividing as they do the time of two whole notes into
three equal accents, correctly express the element of
three in the ratio. The metrical ratio here expressed,
then, is two against three, the equivalent of the interval
of a fifth in tone; while the time-value of the notes employed against each other form a ratio of four against
nine, the equivalent of a major ninth in tone. The poly-
interval thus formed proves to be the interval of a fifth
set over against the interval of a major ninth. It will be
seen how, by following the suggestions offered, any
metre may be used to express any desired numerical
element in any ratio, how different time-systems are
employed against each other in doing so, and how the
length of time necessary in the formation of certain
complicated ratios may be greatly reduced at will. This
subject of the combinations of time and metre might be
much further elaborated. Such elaboration, however, is
not necessary to an understanding of the subject of
metre alone.

6. *Tempo*

The third element of rhythm that remains to be considered is tempo. And it is proposed to apply to this element also the same principles that have already been applied to time and metre. After what has been said, the matter will not be difficult.

Tempo presupposes a given time-system and a given metre. The tempo is slow when a time-unit, say a whole note, is held for a relatively long period, and all the other units take their proportional time. When a shorter time period is taken as a base, the tempo is faster. Often the tempo of a piece is left to the discretion of the performer. Sometimes, however, a composer wishes to indicate the exact speed with which he expects his music to be played; and he is enabled to do this accurately by indicating by the index number of a standard metronome what time should be allowed to a given unit. Thus, M. M. 60 indicates that the metronome beats sixty times to the minute, or one to the second; M. M. 100 represents a correspondingly higher speed, etc. Each one of such beats is the equivalent of a note of designated length, half, quarter, etc. The range of the accepted standard metronome is from 40 to 208 beats to the minute. It is understood, of course, that the use of the metronome suggested here is to set exact rates of speed, not that music should be practised to the accompaniment of a metronome.

In current musical practice the tempo of a given piece

❋❋❋❋❋❋❋❋❋❋❋❋❋❋❋❋❋❋❋❋❋❋❋❋❋❋❋❋❋❋❋❋

is the same for all the parts that are being played simultaneously, and it is likely to be the same, if not for the
entire piece, at least for a passage of considerable length.
If the tempo is changed within a given piece, there is no
system determining the ratio between the consecutive
tempi. Usually the relative speed of two portions is not
evenly accurately designated, but merely indicated by
the general captions, fast, slow; or *allegro, adagio*. In all
the cases thus far cited the changes begin abruptly at
the designated point. Sometimes, however, the caption
"accelerando" indicates that the speed is to be gradually
increased, or *"ritardando"* indicates that it is to be gradually diminished; in either case the rate of change is
left to the taste of the performer.

Applying now the principles of relating time to musical tone, we see at once that if a given tempo, say
M. M. 24, is taken as a base, a tempo of M. M. 48 represents the octave, and M. M. 96 the octave next higher.
The interval of a fifth is represented in tempo by the
ratio M. M. 72, against the octave 48; the interval of a
third by 120 against 96, etc. It is convenient to take a
theoretical base, like 24, lower than is represented on
the metronome, so that its multiples need not mount to
too high a figure. The number 24 is arbitrary, being
chosen to avoid fractions in the tempo scale. If 30 were
chosen as a base, the number of beats per second of the
metronome would equal the vibrations per second of
the tone C of sixteen vibrations, carried down five octaves to a subaudible C. The fractions incurred in the

resulting scale could be accurately determined and marked on an ordinary metronome.

If we wish to use tempo as melody, we have but to establish the tempo value of various tones, and change them as the piece progresses. If a given tone, say the ninth in the series of partials, gives a tempo that is too high for our purpose, 216, it is possible to place it an octave lower, at 108, or even, if desired, at 54. In this way any tone can be brought within practicable limits of the tempo scale. (See tempo scales at the end of this chapter.)

This use of consecutive changes of tempo is of course no new thing; it is the mathematical ratio between tempi that has not been systematized. It can be observed in current practice that when the relations between successive tempi do not follow a simple ratio, but are accidental and arbitrary, the result is felt to be rhythmically rough. Conversely, I am convinced that further investigation would confirm my own experiments, which show that when successive tempi, as chosen by the best conductors, give an impression of smoothness, the conductors have actually, though probably unconsciously, chosen a ratio that is demonstrably simple.

The further application of this system to the purpose of harmonic effect is now self-evident. We have but to use different tempi simultaneously in different parts, choosing and relating them properly according to the tempo scale. The tempi of a new chord are begun simultaneously at a signal from the leader's baton. It is obvious that when more than one tempo is used simultaneously, the number of units of the quicker tempo will be increased in proportion so that musical sections will end simultaneously. Thus, if two tempi were running together, one at M. M. 48, the other at M. M. 96, and both in the same metre, the conductor's beat would represent one measure of the former, while the same beat would represent two measures of the latter. (See Example 24.)

EXAMPLE 24

One reason that different tempi running together would be an advantage is the undoubted difference in feeling between fast notes in a slow tempo, and the notes in a fast tempo, or the reverse. The difference in underlying rate of speed is in some manner evident to the listener, and the mood of a slow movement is different from that of a fast one. The use of different simultaneous tempi in a duet or quartet in opera, for instance, would enable each of the characters to express his individual mood; such a system might effectively be

93

applied to the famous quartet from *Rigoletto,* in which
each of the characters is expressing a different emotion.
It will be well at this point to examine the use that may
be made of accelerated and diminished speed in tempo.
Considered in terms of tone, accelerated or diminished
tempo would, of course, represent a sliding tone going
upwards or downwards in the scale. In the practical
handling of such changing tempo, two factors have to
be considered: the two rates of tempo at the beginning
and end of the slide have to be chosen accurately to
harmonize with the tempo scale being used; and the
time assigned for accomplishing the change has to be
accurately indicated. If we were to represent graphically
different tempi by horizontal lines running parallel,
the higher ones representing higher rates of speed, accelerated speed would be represented by a sliding line
from one of the horizontal lines to another higher one.
The angle of the slanting line would be determined (1)
by the height to be attained and (2) by the amount of
time, measured horizontally, granted for reaching the
height. Thus, a change from M. M. 48 to M. M. 96, if
accomplished in three measures, would be represented
by an easy slant, while the same change, if accomplished
in one measure, would be represented by a steep one.
If more than one different angle, to continue the figure,
be used simultaneously, the problem is simplified by the
consideration that the slanting lines can be made to
reach points that are distant from each other according
to a simple arithmetical ratio. Thus in the next example

horizontal lines represent steady rates of tempo, vertical lines metrical divisions, and slanting lines parts of tempo accelerating at three different rates of speed. It will be seen that the two lower slanting lines are arranged so that at any given point in the vertical lines one slanting line is twice as far from the original starting-point as the other. At the end of one measure the first slanting line arrives at M. M. 72, while the other arrives at M. M. 60; at the end of two measures they arrive respectively at M. M. 96 and M. M. 72. (See Example 25.)

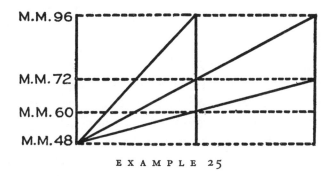

E X A M P L E   25

Should it be desired, the slanting line could be broken into two parts making an angle, the first element of which might be steeper and the second easier, or vice versa. In any case the change would be accomplished at an exact instant chosen. Diminished tempo, of course, would be similarly represented by a straight or broken line slanting downwards.

For practical purposes, care would have to be exercised in the use of sliding tempo, in order to control the relation between tones in a sliding part with those in another part being played at the same time: a composer would have to know, in other words, what tones in a part with rising tempo would be struck simultaneously with other tones in a part of, say, fixed tempo, and this from considerations of harmony. There would usually be no absolute coincidence, but the tones which would be struck at approximately the same time could be calculated.

When we come to apply the system of relative tempo according to the laws of counterpoint, we have only to observe the familiar rules as worked out in tonal counterpoint. Whether the changes of tempo be abrupt or sliding, the tempo of any given part must be regulated with reference to the tempo just preceding it in the same part, as well as by the tempi of the simultaneous parts. If fixed tempi are used, the tempo of one part may continue over two periods, while that of another part is changed at the second period; or, if one change is a step up, to a quicker tempo, the other may be down, to a slower. One tempo may remain constant while another slides up or down, or both may slide in opposite directions, etc. If properly handled, the changes in tempo will bear a close analogy to the tonal changes in counterpoint, and the distinction from the harmonic use of tempo will be maintained. (See Example 26.)

A further use of tempo is in its combination with

EXAMPLE 26

97

EXAMPLE 26

time or metre. By the correct application of a change of
tempo, a change of the rhythmic key of time or metre
can be made. For instance, if a quarter-note at M. M.
96 equals C, it is evident that if the tempo is changed to
M. M. 72, the quarter-note will be of different value—
namely, the equivalent of G. In this way the key tone
of the whole time or metric system can be changed at
will, and many simplifications of practice can be made.
If, for instance, the rhythmic chord of C (in the ratio
of 4:5:6) has been struck, and it is desired to strike
the chord of F, this can be done in the key of C only by
the use of three-sixteenths notes against three-twentieths
notes against eighth-notes. If, however, the tempo be
changed from M. M. 96 to M. M. 64, the chord of F
can be expressed by quarter-notes against fifth-notes
against sixth-notes, since by means of the change of
tempo the key will have been changed to that of F.

7. Scales of Rhythm

Since our appreciation has been limited, for the most
part, to the simplest rhythms, and since it is difficult to
play accurately more complex ones, it is necessary to
form rhythmic scales of the simplest possible ratios.
Therefore, instead of using the ratios of customary sys-

tems of temperament upon which to base rhythmic scales, we employ the simplest overtone ratios which can be found to approximate each interval. The series of ratios upon which these scales are formed, then, is as follows:

$$
\begin{array}{lll}
C:C & = & 1:1 \\
C:C\sharp & = & 14:15 \ (C:D\flat = 15:16) \\
C:D & = & 8:9 \\
C:E\flat & = & 5:6 \\
C:E & = & 4:5 \\
C:F & = & 3:4 \\
C:G\flat & = & 5:7 \\
C:G & = & 2:3 \\
C:A\flat & = & 5:8 \\
C:A & = & 3:5 \\
C:B\flat & = & 4:7 \\
C:B & = & 8:15 \\
C:C & = & 1:2 \\
\end{array}
$$

TIME

In the scale of time-values a quarter-note is taken as the equivalent of C. The reason for this is evident—a low C in tone is produced by sixteen vibrations per second. If this C be carried down two octaves, the result is a subaudible C of four vibrations per second. If the time-value of a whole note is taken to be one second, four quarter-notes will be produced in one second, just as four vibrations will produce a subaudible C. The corresponding time-values of the other tones of the scale are such that the number of times a given note is contained in a whole note will equal the number of vibrations per

99

second of the corresponding tone, on a base of C equal to four vibrations. Thus, C sharp has four and two-sevenths vibrations per second; and it will be found that a seven-thirtieths note, which is the corresponding time-value of C sharp, will be contained in a whole note four and two-sevenths times; in other words, four seventh-thirtieths notes plus one fifteenth-note (a fifteenth-note is two-sevenths of a seven-thirtieths note) will equal a whole note. It will also be seen that the ratio from C to any other tone of the scale will be found, in time, by using quarter-notes to express the numerical element of the ratio that equals C, and notes of the time-value given to fill the remaining numerical element. Thus, the ratio between C and C sharp is 14: 15. If fourteen quarter-notes are placed over against fifteen seven-thirtieths notes, the ratio will be correctly expressed.

Since the time of a single vibration grows smaller with each succeeding higher tone, the length of notes of corresponding time-value grows shorter as the scale is ascended, until an octave up from the fundamental a note of half the fundamental time-value is reached. In the following scale will be found the correspondences between tones of the chromatic scale and notes of various time-values. (See Example 27.)

The meaning of the columns in the foregoing chart is self-evident, except possibly that of the right-hand column. This column gives the method of notating the various time-values given. A reference back to the table

Intervals from C.	Ratios from C.	Tones of Chromatic Scale.		Corresponding Time Value
		C	=	4th note (♩)
Augmented unison	14 : 15	C sharp	=	7|30ths note (♩..)
Major second	8 : 9	D	=	2|9ths note (♩)
Minor third	5 : 6	E flat	=	5|24ths note (♩♪)
Major third	4 : 5	E	=	5th note (♩)
Perfect fourth	3 : 4	F	=	3|16ths note (♩.)
Diminished fifth	5 : 7	G flat	=	5|28ths note (♩♪)
Perfect fifth	2 : 3	G	=	6th note (♩)
Minor sixth	5 : 8	A flat	=	5|32nds note (♪♪)
Major sixth	3 : 5	A	=	3|20ths note (♪.)
Minor seventh	4 : 7	B flat	=	7th note (♩)
Major seventh	8 : 15	B	=	2|5ths note (♩)
Perfect octave	1 : 2	C	=	8th note (♪)

E X A M P L E 2 7

of different-shaped notes will show the reason for the various shapes employed.

In spite of the ratios being simplified as far as possible, some of the time equivalents are complex, and it is likely that until we develop further in rhythmic appreciation, only the simpler ratios of the scale will be used. If C were made a variant instead of being confined to a quarter-note, simpler kinds of notes might be employed to express certain ratios, although the ratios themselves would be unchanged. The intervals of the scale that such a procedure would effect, and their rhythmic expression, are shown on page 103.

METRE

To avoid complications of time a standard time of quarter-notes is made the basis of all the metres here employed. The formation of a metrical scale in which C equals a constant metre entails consideration of such metres as are too complex for practical purposes. Therefore the table here given concerns interval ratios in which C corresponds to a variable metre. For example, the interval C: C sharp may be represented by a system of two simultaneous groups of 210 quarter-notes, divided in one voice into fourteen measure of $^{15}\!/\!_4$ metre, as against fifteen measures of $^{14}\!/\!_4$ metre in another voice. It will be noted that in this example—a 14:15 ratio— the 14 factor is represented by groups of fifteen notes, while the 15 factor employs groups of fourteen notes. The least number of notes that will fully exemplify this interval ratio is the product of these two numbers, or 210. Such numerical cross-relations hold good throughout.

If it were necessary to form this interval with C as a constant metre, which would be a metre of $^2\!/\!_4$, the

Intervals	Ratios	Specific Intervals in the Chromatic Scale of C	Rhythmic Expressions of Ratios with C as a Variant
Augmented unison	14 : 15	C : C♯	14 14th-notes : 15 15th-notes
Minor third	5 : 6	C : E♭	5 5th-notes : 6 6th-notes
Perfect fourth	3 : 4	C : F	3 3rd-notes : 4 4th-notes
Diminished fifth	5 : 7	C : G♭	5 5th-notes : 7 7th-notes
Minor sixth	5 : 8	C : A♭	5 5th-notes : 8 8th-notes
Major sixth	3 : 5	C : A	3 3rd-notes : 5 5th-notes

expression would be fourteen measures of $\frac{2}{4}$ metre, set over against fifteen measures of $\dfrac{2\frac{1}{7}}{49\text{-}225}$ metre. This is a metre of $2\frac{1}{7}$, since an accented note will be followed by one and one-seventh unaccented notes. One measure of such metre will contain two 49–225ths notes plus one 7–225ths note, the latter kind of note being one-seventh the length of the former; and the length of time of the whole measure is such that it is contained two and one-seventh times in a measure of $\frac{2}{4}$ metre. Both the kind of metre and the length of the measure, then, express the fraction two and one-seventh, which is the correct expression of C sharp, if C equals the number 2.

The almost insurmountable complexity of this procedure is now sufficiently evident. It would be interesting, though, to hear such rhythms cut on a player-piano roll. The table of metrical equivalents with C as a variant follows on page 105.

The meaning of the columns is self-evident, except perhaps that of the right-hand column. This column shows the number of quarter-notes that must be passed over before the metrical ratio in question is completed.

TEMPO

The scales of tempo are self-explanatory. The base of 24 equal to C is arbitrary, but 30 equal to C, which is correct theoretically, gives more unpractical fractions,

Intervals of the Chromatic Scale		Ratios and Metrical Expression	Ratio Lengths in Quarter-notes
Perfect unison	C : C	1 measure of 2/4 metre : 1 of 2/4 metre	(2)
Augmented unison	C : C♯	14 measures of 15/4 metre : 15 of 14/4 metre	(210)
Major second	C : D	8 measures of 9/4 metre : 9 of 8/4 metre	(72)
Minor third	C : E♭	5 measures of 6/4 metre : 6 of 5/4 metre	(30)
Major third	C : E	4 measures of 5/4 metre : 5 of 4/4 metre	(20)
Perfect fourth	C : F	3 measures of 4/4 metre : 4 of 3/4 metre	(12)
Diminished fifth	C : G♭	5 measures of 7/4 metre : 7 of 5/4 metre	(35)
Perfect fifth	C : G	2 measures of 3/4 metre : 3 of 2/4 metre	(6)
Minor sixth	C : A♭	5 measures of 8/4 metre : 8 of 5/4 metre	(40)
Major sixth	C : A	3 measures of 5/4 metre : 5 of 3/4 metre	(15)
Minor seventh	C : B♭	4 measures of 7/4 metre : 7 of 4/4 metre	(28)
Major seventh	C : B	8 measures of 15/4 metre : 15 of 8/4 metre	(120)
Perfect octave	C : C	1 measure of 4/4 metre : 2 of 2/4 metre	(4)

as is shown below. Equivalent numbers are suggested here for such fractions as are produced by using 24 as a base. It will be noted that the scale as given begins from the octave of the fundamental—namely, 48.

Ratios from C	Tones of Chromatic Scale	Equivalent M.M.Nos.	Second Equivalents (to Avoid Fractions)
	C	= 48	
14 : 15	C♯	= 51 3/7	(C♯ as 5th partial of A = 50—ratio from C, 24 : 25)
8 : 9	D	= 54	
5 : 6	E♭	= 57 2/5	(E♭ as 3rd underpartial of B♭ = 56—ratio from C, 6 : 7)
4 : 5	E	= 60	
3 : 4	F	= 64	
5 : 7	G♭	= 67 1/5	(F♯ as 11th partial of C = 66—ratio from C, 8 : 11)
2 : 3	G	= 72	
5 : 8	A♭	= 76 4/5	(G♯ as 5th partial of E = 75—ratio from C, 16 : 25)
3 : 5	A	= 80	
4 : 7	B♭	= 84	
8 : 15	B	= 90	
1 : 2	C	= 96	

The ratios from C of the second equivalent M. M. numbers are more complex than those of the first equivalents; but, owing to the base of the scale (24), produce whole numbers, whereas the ratios of the first equivalents produce fractions.

Below is given another tempo scale, on a base of 30.

This base is acoustically more correct, but the scale
formed from it contains more difficult fractions than
that formed from the base 24. The scale as given begins
on the octave C = 60.

Ratios from C	Tones of Chromatic Scale		Equivalent M. M. Numbers
	C	=	60
14 : 15	C♯	=	64 2/7
8 : 9	D	=	67 1/2
5 : 6	E♭	=	72
4 : 5	E	=	75
3 : 4	F	=	80
5 : 7	G♭	=	84
2 : 3	G	=	90
5 : 8	A♭	=	96
3 : 5	A	=	100
4 : 7	B♭	=	105
8 : 15	B	=	112 1/2
1 : 2	C	=	120

Although at first sight the fractions in this scale do
not seem more difficult to handle than in the scale
based on 24, it will be seen that two of the fractions are
used in the expression of the tones D and B of the
major scale, whereas the fractions incurred in the scale
based on 24 are in the less-used chromatic tones; and
also that whereas equivalents can be found for the latter, for the former there are none possible, since there
is but one correct method of obtaining ratios for the
major scale. As has been stated before, however, the
numbers and fractions contained in this scale can be
accurately determined and marked on a metronome,

if desired, thus making the scale available for practical purposes; or the fractions might be struck out as being too fine to be perceived by the auditor, and the nearest whole numbers taken instead.

Although the rhythmical values suggested in the foregoing scales are for the most part new, simpler cross-rhythms, more particularly those formed by different note-durations, have of course been used by many composers. Chopin in notating his *rubato* improvisations hit on some extraordinary combinations; Brahms developed individual forms of syncopation; Scriabine carried a Chopinesque variety of cross-rhythm a step further than Chopin; Stravinsky utilized irregular metres and cross-accents.

Charles Ives, however, has gone furthest in weaving webs of counter-rhythms. Chords of rhythm are suggested in his works, and he builds up musical moods which rely on rhythmical subtleties to an even greater extent than on tonal elements for their effect.

PART III

Chord-Formation

❀❀❀❀❀❀❀❀❀❀

1. *Building Chords from Different Intervals*

In the conventional study of harmony the process of explaining the method of building up chords is to point out that they are formed, in their original positions, by the addition of intervals of a third, one on top of another. Thus, a "common chord" or major triad is found to contain a major third underneath, on which has been superimposed a minor third. A minor chord is formed in reverse manner, by adding a major third on top of a minor third. A diminished triad is formed by the use of two minor thirds together, while an augmented triad is built from two major thirds. When additional material is desired, another major or minor third is added to either of the four triads, making what is called a seventh chord, as the outside interval so formed will always be a seventh. Certain seventh chords have been preferred for frequent use, such as the "dominant" seventh chord, formed by two minor thirds above a major one. The reason for this is doubtless that such a chord is actually formed by the overtone series (fourth to seventh partials, inclusive). The use of all other forms of seventh chords, however, as well as ninth chords, which are formed by adding still another third to a seventh chord, is general in contemporary music. No particular reason for building chords in thirds rather than other intervals is customarily given; but the reason becomes evident in the light of the interpretation of the history of chord usage, given in the first chapter. In early times the first few overtone intervals, fifths, fourths, and octaves, were regarded as the foundation of intervals, and the musical theory of those times permitted only fifths and octaves as points of rest, while thirds and sixths, or any other intervals, were resolved to the "perfect" intervals. Thus it can be seen that the harmony of that time, which was considered incidental to the counterpoint, was built on fifths and their inversion, fourths. Later, when thirds and their inversion, sixths, came to be considered concordant, they were made the basis of chords, and this is the system still taught. The overtones represented are the next removed from those forming fifths and fourths— namely, from the fourth partial to the seventh, the overtones there being spaced as thirds, first a major third, then two minor thirds. It is only by leaving out the eighth partial that the ninth, necessary for the formation of a ninth chord, may be said to fall among the possibilities of chords built in thirds. The simplest theoretical explanation of seventh chords other than the dominant, and ninth chords other than the dominant, seems to be to regard them as polychords, with tones in common, formed by closely related harmonies. Thus, the tonic major seventh chord (such as C, E, G,

B) can be considered a combination of the tonic triad (C, E, G) with the mediant triad (E, G, B).

Since we have seen the development of the use of chords from the simplest ones in ancient times, through somewhat more complex ones later, and still more complex ones in present-day music, all following the overtone series on upwards, it seems inevitable that the system of building up chords must eventually include the next overtones after those related in thirds— namely, from the seventh overtone upwards. There seems to be need of such a system to further the understanding of contemporary material, which has had no adequate theoretical co-ordination, in spite of being in everyday use in composition. It is impossible to explain all modern materials as being further complications of chords built in thirds.

If we are to have a better understanding of the materials possible within the limits of a scale of twelve tones to an octave, we must have three systems, rather than one; and these three systems, being entirely similar in their working-out, can be readily co-ordinated. The first system is of chords built in fifths and their inversions, fourths, and diminished fifths. This was suggested as a beginning by the ancients, was left during the classical period, and now is being investigated by composers such as Schönberg and Rudhyar. This discovery on their part of the possibilities of a system in fifths seems to fill in a historical gap, bringing an ancient idea forward to its final use, rather than a step forward in the line of progress, as the perfect intervals are the most primary of the overtone series. It is interesting to observe that the triad or common chord of a system of fifths (such as C, G, D) is in many ways more concordant than the familiar triad in thirds (such as C, E, G), as it is a more open sound, and the resultant sound-complex contains fewer beats. The second system of the three necessary to cover the entire field is the familiar one based on thirds, and their inversions, sixths.

The third system would be based on the next higher overtones after thirds—namely, seconds, both major and minor. Through inversion, sevenths would be included in this system as well. From the seventh partial onwards, a series of major seconds is formed by the overtones; very large seconds at first, then smaller and smaller until between the fifteenth and sixteenth partials a minor second is reached. The overtones from the seventh to the fourteenth partials (if the twelfth, which occurs in a lower octave, is omitted) form a whole-tone scale, which is thus seen to have a sound accoustical foundation. Many of the chords employed by Debussy and others in whole-tone music give the suggestion of being built on major seconds. These chords, however, are rarely bunched together in groups of seconds, but are more often spaced more widely apart.

The use of chords based on clusters of seconds, built

114

as they are on the next reaches of the overtones after thirds, would seem inevitable in the development of music. There is no reason to suppose that the progress along the overtones which has been made from early musical times to the present will suddenly stop. Also, it may be pointed out that the natural spacing of so-called dissonances is as seconds grouped together, as in the overtone series, rather than as sevenths or ninths; since from the time of the entrance of the seventh partial, the first dissonance according to the text-books, the partials travel in ever-narrowing seconds. Groups spaced in seconds may be made to sound very euphonious, particularly if played in conjunction with fundamental chord notes taken from lower in the same overtone series. This blends them together and explains them to the ear. The wider spacing in sevenths and ninths is often desirable, of course, particularly in counterpoint, as it gives the inner parts more space in which to move about. It has probably been from a feeling (perhaps without much investigation) that the parts would be cramped in groups of tones spaced in seconds that more attention has not been given to the possibilities lying in such groups, in which the parts need not be cramped if a study is made of how to proceed with them.

There has been sporadic use of the device of adding a second of some sort to a common chord, with the excuse of "adding colour." This, of course, is not a tenable explanation of why the particular second should be used, and is a confusion of the theory and purpose of music. The purpose of every note in a large chord may be to add colour to the composition as a whole, yet from the standpoint of theory there must be some reason why the chord used was one which, in the way it was handled, would produce colour. To say that in such a group as C, D, E played together the D is a colour-note does not explain why it should be there, nor why another note would not be just as good as a colour-note; it merely gives a name. The same is true when an attempt is made to explain the D as a passing-note played at the same time as the other notes. This also is only a name and is no explanation of why a passing-note, which is distinctly a melodic device, should suddenly without further reason be acceptable in harmony. All attempts which would relegate the D to a secondary position to the C and E beg the question and are a result of trying to explain everything from the standpoint of the axiomatic supremacy of thirds, which standpoint has no tenable foundation. It is far simpler to consider all the notes in any chord as equal and independent, accepting the chord C, D, E as one built on a system of seconds, not as part of the triad of C, unexplainably filled in with an extra note which does not belong to it.

In order to distinguish groups built on seconds from groups built on thirds or fifths, they will hereafter be called tone-clusters.

116

2. *Tone-clusters*

Tone-clusters, then, are chords built from major and minor seconds, which in turn may be derived from the upper reaches of the overtone series and have, therefore, a sound foundation. In building up clusters from seconds, it will be seen that since both major and minor seconds are used, just as major and minor thirds are used in the familiar systems in thirds, there is an exact resemblance between the two systems, and the same amount of potential variety in each. Thus we have the following formula for common triads: major, a major third with a minor third on top; minor, a minor third with a major on top; diminished, two minor thirds; augmented, two major thirds. This formula can be transplanted to the system in seconds, and we arrive at exact equivalents: (1) a major second with

EXAMPLE 28

a minor on top gives us, building from C, the cluster C, D, E flat; (2) a minor second with a major on top —C, D flat, E flat; (3) two minor seconds—C, D flat, E double-flat; (4) two major seconds—C, D, E. These four triads are the basis of all larger clusters, which can have great variety, owing to the many different possible juxtapositions of the triads within larger clusters. (See Example 28.)

When clusters are used alone, large ones often prove less cramped than small ones, as in very small clusters

EXAMPLE 29

used alone there may not be enough room in which to move the parts. (See Example 29.) A running part in clusters may be effective in connexion with chords in other systems. (See Example 30.) Small clusters used

EXAMPLE 30

only occasionally between chords of other systems may be desirable if handled cautiously, particularly in dissonant counterpoint. (See Example 31.) In harmony it

EXAMPLE 31

is often better for the sake of consistency to maintain a whole succession of clusters, once they are begun; since one alone, or even two, may be heard as a mere effect, rather than as an independent and significant procedure, carried with musical logic to its inevitable conclusion.

One reason that a large cluster is a natural reinforcement when played at the same time as a simple chord is that whenever a simple triad is played, the higher overtones of all three tones, which are plainly audible to a sensitive ear, form such a cluster. It would seem that only listeners with very crude hearing can be shocked at the sound of either a cluster or any natural dissonance, since a musical ear would already be familiar with the sound through hearing it as overtones of familiar chords.

On the piano smaller clusters of any sort are playable,

but larger ones are more easily played if they are either chromatic, including all the keys between specific outer limits, or all on black keys, or all on white keys. This forms pentatonic clusters on the black keys, five different cluster chords of the same length being possible. On the white keys seven different cluster chords of the same length may be formed, and major, minor, or various modal scales may be used. There is less possible variety on the piano than with the orchestra, where clusters are at their best; nevertheless, there is more variety than would appear at first, made possible by changing the length of the clusters, as well as by their innumerable relationships to chords in other systems. A sense of monotony which may be felt by a listener through first hearing successions of clusters soon vanishes when the ear begins hearing the subtle distinctions between the different placements of major and minor seconds in the inner parts, just as it does now with thirds. (See Example 28.) In orchestral use we have all the possible variety of large clusters which are neither all chromatic nor all diatonic, but constructed from a consistent building up of diversified smaller cluster triads. (See Example 28.)

In familiar theory there are certain well-known ways of building with musical material, such as by use of chord-connexions, contrapuntal melodic relationship, canonic imitation, retrograde, thematic structure, etc. All of these methods may be applied to clusters, which also bring with them, however, some new processes of their own.

A characteristic quality of harmony is the possibility of movement within outside tones; that is, in changes of harmony the inner voices usually move to tones which were contained within the outer limits of the tones of the previous chord. But so long as our scale is limited to half-tone intervals, it is obviously impossible to shift tones within the outer limits of a chromatic cluster, except through interchanging the parts. The cluster must be treated like a single unit, as a single tone is treated. All movement must be up or down the scale, as in melody.

(a)

Owing to the difficulty of reading such clusters, it is suggested that they be rotated by means of a single note running through from the highest to the lowest note of the cluster. The above cluster would then be presented thus:

(b)

EXAMPLE 32

A cluster, obviously, must be measured to show its size, and this may easily be done as intervals are measured, using the distance between the outside members of the clusters. Thus, a cluster of three consecutive chromatic tones may be called a cluster major second, a cluster of four consecutive tones may be called a cluster minor third, etc. (See Example 32.) The important tones, the ones that are most plainly heard, are those of the outer edges of a given cluster, just as we hear best the soprano and bass of a four-part chord. Given a series of clusters of the same interval, we can conveniently designate them by the names of their lowest tones.

There are two ways of using tone-clusters for melodic effect. One is to move clusters of the same interval up and down the scale, just as tones are moved in melody. (See Example 33.) The other is to shift the size

EXAMPLE 33

of the interval as the cluster moves. In this latter case the outer tones move independently of each other, making two simultaneous melodies which must be related to each other contrapuntally. (See Example 34.) Musical patterns can be made by combining the two methods into sequences, etc.

In the consideration of tone-clusters it is useful to

EXAMPLE 34

distinguish between those whose outer tones form a consonant interval, and those whose outer tones form a dissonance. The greater simplicity of the former is readily appreciated by the ear.

Just as it is possible to use successive clusters for melodic effect, so we can use simultaneous clusters for harmonic effect. If the clusters which form the units are of the same size, it is logical to group them just as tones are grouped in a chord. Thus, if we form a chord of three simultaneous clusters, the lowest cluster extending from C to E, the middle cluster from G to B, and the highest from E to G sharp, the lowest tones of the three clusters added together would form the common major chord of C; and the highest tones added, the common chord of E. The whole cluster chord, then, might be called a common major cluster chord; and, since we use the lowest tone to designate chords, it might be called the common cluster chord of C, with clusters of a third. (See Example 35.) Clusters of any interval could, of course, be used. Care should be taken to see that clusters are so spaced as to be distinct. The

123

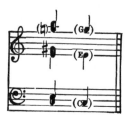

EXAMPLE 35

larger the cluster, the wider must the spacing be. Thus, as an exercise in the use of cluster chords, we might start with a composition in tonal harmony and translate it into corresponding cluster chords, naming each tone-cluster from its lowest tone, and spacing the clusters

EXAMPLE 36

as the circumstances might require. (See Example 36.)
If, however, the clusters were not of the same size, the
combination of several such clusters would make a
cluster chord, but not one that would correspond in
the same way to a tonal harmony. (See Example 37.)

E X A M P L E 37

In this case the outer tones of the clusters would form
an ordinary chord.

Contrapuntal effect may be introduced in several
ways. One is to translate the familiar devices of tonal
counterpoint into the new medium of tone-clusters,
keeping the clusters of the same size throughout. (See

E X A M P L E 38

Example 38.) If tone-clusters of different sizes are used as the units of successive cluster chords, there is an effect of two melodies in each of the clusters, and this is a contrapuntal consideration. Thus, if we have two groups of simultaneous clusters which successively change their size, the result is a problem of four-part counterpoint. (See Example 39.) The two methods we have mentioned may also be used together.

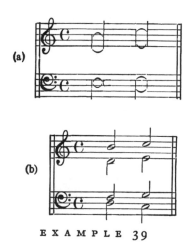

EXAMPLE 39

All the tone-clusters of which we have thus far spoken are what we might call fixed; that is, it has been assumed that the several tones are struck simultaneously. Clusters that do in a certain sense move are, however, quite possible, and it is interesting to consider the various ways in which such movement can be introduced.

For ease of reading, the time of sustained tones might be represented by means of a black line which would run horizontally along the staff position of the note as long as the tone in question was held. The time of added notes would be represented as usual. This would obviate the necessity of tying tones. By employing this method the above moving cluster would be notated as follows:

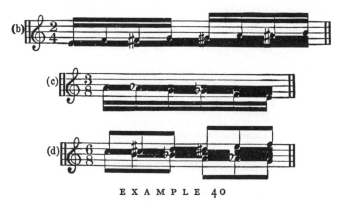

EXAMPLE 40

One way is to play the tones of a cluster in quick succession, holding them as they are played. This is a cluster of an essentially different kind from one fixed, for although it is possible to regard the movement simply as a means of arriving at a fixed cluster of a larger interval, it is also possible, and especially interesting, to regard the cluster as one of changing size, like an

127

angle whose sides are projected to greater and greater
length. There are three ways of thus spreading a cluster: one is to begin with the lowest tone and go up;
another to begin with the highest tone and go down;
and the third to begin with the middle of the cluster
and spread it in both directions at once. (See Example 40.)

The reverse also is possible. A cluster may be reduced
by beginning with a cluster and leaving off tones, beginning with the lowest tone; or doing the same, beginning with the highest tone; or by leaving off tones
simultaneously from top and bottom, until only the
middle is left. (See Example 41.) A combination move-

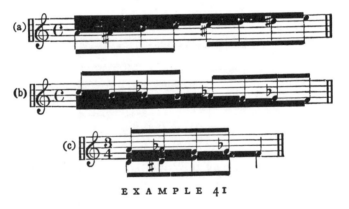

EXAMPLE 41

ment is likewise possible by beginning with a tone-
cluster of a given interval, say a fifth, and then adding
tones at one edge at the same time that they are let
go at the other, with the result that the cluster keeps

its original interval of a fifth while shifting up or down the scale. (See Example 42.)

EXAMPLE 42

Another variation possible in the treatment of moving clusters is to have the rate of expansion or contraction of one edge of a cluster different from the rate at the other edge. (See Example 43.) This method of treatment is applicable to all the varieties of clusters in which the movement is twofold.

EXAMPLE 43

In all moving clusters, as opposed to fixed, we note that a different method of treatment is called for, for the essential thing about them is the fact of their movement itself, and not the attainment of a fixed cluster as a whole. Another point to note is that when clusters shift gradually at both edges and in the same direction, the progression is parallel and suggests homophony; whereas when their expanding or contracting

129

or shifting results in oblique or contrary motion, the effect is, on the contrary, more polyphonic.

If we consider moving clusters as units, it can be seen how they may be combined into larger units of harmony. If we begin two moving clusters at a fixed interval apart and expand them at the same rate and in the same direction, they may be said to be in that interval. (See Example 44.) From intervals thus built

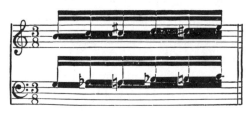

EXAMPLE 44

up it is a simple thing to form chords, and with chords as material the different applications of ordinary tonal harmony can find their analogy.

Effects of counterpoint in moving clusters are also obtainable. We remember that in tonal counterpoint the so-called second species is obtained when a tone in one part is held while two tones are sounded one after the other in a corresponding part. To produce this in moving clusters we may have one part moving continuously while the other part moves at a given interval distant, and then breaks, to complete the unit at a different interval. (See Example 45.) From this as a sim-

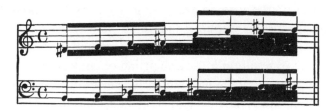

EXAMPLE 45

ple beginning it is possible to build up a complete system of counterpoint in moving clusters.

In the effects of counterpoint just mentioned, the intervals are always moving in the same direction. If,

EXAMPLE 46

however, the moving parts be in contrary directions, the effect is contrapuntal in a different way. The same is true if the rate of speed of two related clusters is different, resulting in a combination of angles that is of its nature contrapuntal. Similarly, the combination of a fixed and a moving cluster gives a contrapuntal effect. (See Example 46.) Furthermore, a combination of two methods is possible. We can, for example, take second species counterpoint as a base, continuing the movement of one part in one direction, while the other part moves parallel up to a certain point and is then reversed in direction. (See Example 47.) This is only a

EXAMPLE 47

single and a very simple example to suggest the wide variety with which different methods of producing contrapuntal effect can be applied.

A method of using clusters that has no counterpart in traditional counterpoint and harmony is to begin

EXAMPLE 48

132

with a sufficiently large cluster and then leave out the middle part, with the result that two smaller clusters remain. (See Example 48.) In very large original clusters, there is a possibility of dividing into a greater number of smaller ones, and of spacing these at will, so as to make, if desired, a cluster chord. And the reverse can equally well be accomplished by beginning with a group of smaller clusters and then filling in the gaps until a large cluster results. (See Example 49.) The

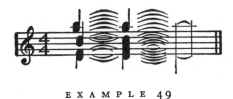

EXAMPLE 49

production of a chord by adding tones from the bass upwards until the desired chord is complete is well known in musical practice under the name of arpeggiation; and the opposite method, which we may call subtraction, is known in some instances, although it is seldom employed. In its use the tones of a chord are subtracted one by one, until only the lowest is left. These methods of building up and pulling down, by addition and subtraction, are applicable also to clusters. If the outline of a cluster is filled in from several different points, the cluster will be thought of as essentially fixed, even though the notes are not struck simultaneously, and this for the reason that the listener

133

recognizes the intention to fill in completely an exact interval. We may think of it, then, as another kind of cluster. At any and every point before completing such a cluster we have a new harmony, which must be built up with consideration for harmonic principles. If the desire is to give an impression of consonance, it is well to build a foundation of consonant harmonies first, before adding the necessary dissonant tones. (See Example 50.) And the reverse, of course, is also true. If

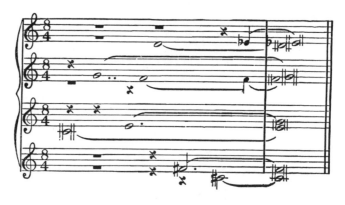

EXAMPLE 50

we fill in the larger outline of a cluster by adding several tones at a time, the relation of these tones may be a polyharmonic consideration. (See Example 51.) Reverse the principle of addition in its various methods, and we have different ways of applying the principle of subtraction. But here it will be noted that the aim in subtraction is to leave out, not related tones, but

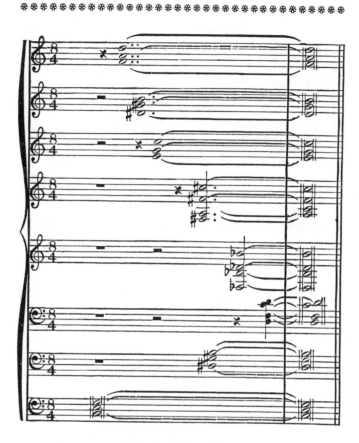

EXAMPLE 51

those which will leave related tones remaining to give harmonic or polyharmonic effect. (See Example 52.)

Yet another variation in the method of building up clusters is to begin with a chord and then to fill in the requisite tones simultaneously. The chord then passes

135

EXAMPLE 52

at once into a cluster. (See Example 53.) And a cluster, in its turn, may be reduced to a chord instantane-

EXAMPLE 53

ously by a reversal of the same method. (See Example 54.)

In forming diatonic cluster chords two methods are possible in relation to the tonality or tonalities which it is desired to employ. To maintain simplicity we can, for one thing, confine ourselves to tones that appear

EXAMPLE 54

136

in the scale of one key. Thus, if clusters of a fifth begin with C and G respectively in the key of C, all the tones of the clusters may appear in the original key of C major. (See Example 55.) Or, if we wish to use the

EXAMPLE 55

polytonal method, we may make our clusters from the tones of related keys. For example, if we have two clusters of the interval of a seventh, beginning with C and G respectively, the C cluster may include an F natural, since that is in the key of C, whereas the G cluster may include an F sharp, which is a distinctive tone of the key of G. (See Example 56.)

There are infinitely more ways of using clusters, but the working-out of details cannot be treated of here,

EXAMPLE 56

any more than the details of treatment of the new rhythmical suggestions. Any composer sufficiently interested will probably wish to work out such details himself, and it is hoped, in putting forth the present outline, that different musicians may take interest in working on the innumerable details of the various subjects. The detailed manner in which each material may be handled is hardly a matter to be decided beforehand and forced upon composers; each one has the right and desire to manage his own materials in such a fashion that they become the best vehicle for his own musical expression.

To disregard the subject of materials, however, does not make for a personal style, or for perfection or freedom of expression. Musical emotions are never so spontaneous as when the forms through which they manifest themselves are so well known to the composer as to be subconscious and can be delicately adjusted to the particular situation. The emotions of a listener with fine perception can never be entirely pleasurable or satisfactory if the composition he is hearing contains crudities of which he cannot but be emotionally as well as intellectually aware.

For the sake of the exquisiteness of emotion which music may express, as well as for the sake of perfection of the music itself, therefore, there is a place for the formalization and co-ordination of different contemporary musical resources by means of their common relationship with the overtone series, which, although it forms a mathematical, acoustical, and historical gauge, is not merely a matter of arithmetic, theory, and pedantry, but is itself a living essence from which musicality springs.

Following are definitions of some of the terms used in *New Musical Resources*. Terms used which are not included here are defined in the text.

CANON: Composition in which the process of imitation is continued throughout. The imitation may start from the same tone as the first part, or the imitation may start from a different tone, but follow the same melodic pattern as the first melody.

CHORD: A group of at least three different tones sounded together.

COUNTERPOINT: The relationship of simultaneous melodies to each other.

CROSS-RHYTHM (or counter-rhythm): Two or more parts playing different systems of rhythms against each other.

HARMONY: The connexion of a succession of chords, or the principle of relating simultaneous tones.

IMITATION: The process of repeating in one part a short melody, or motif, which has just previously occurred in another part.

INTERVAL: The distance between two tones, usually measured from the lowest tone. Following is a table of the most familiar intervals and their names:

C : C	Perfect unison
C : C♯	Augmented unison
C : D♭	Minor second
C : D	Major second
C : D♯	Augmented second
C : E♭	Minor third
C : E	Major third
C : F	Perfect fourth
C : F♯	Augmented fourth
C : G♭	Diminished fifth
C : G	Perfect fifth
C : G♯	Augmented fifth
C : A♭	Minor sixth
C : A	Major sixth
C : A♯	Augmented sixth
C : B♭	Minor seventh
C : B	Major seventh
C : C	Perfect octave

INVERSION: The process of removing the lowest tone in a chord or interval, and replacing it an octave higher.

MELODY: Any series of successive, related tones. (The idea that to be called a melody, a succession of tones must be tuneful, or immediately pleasurable, is to be avoided; in this work any succession of related tones is considered to embody the melodic principle, and to have potential value, whether enjoyed immediately or not.)

MUSIC: What constitutes music is a question on which authorities differ; according to some theorists, only works following certain rules of procedure should be called music; in which case most modern experiment and all primitive outpourings of tonal expression would be without a name. In this work the term "music" is used to refer to all attempts man has made or may make to fashion tonal and rhythmical material. The question will not then be to decide what is music and what is not music, but to decide which music is preferable in quality.

NINTH CHORD: A chord in which the outside interval is a ninth.

POLYPHONY: The sounding of many voices, or melodies, together. Polyphony refers to counterpoint, but may also be used to indicate freely moving parts which do not follow the rules of counterpoint.

RESOLUTION: The process of following a tone which produces a dissonance, by a tone which is consonant with the remaining tones. The usual method of resolution has been to follow the dissonant tone by a tone which is a whole or half step removed down the scale.

ROOT-POSITION: The root is the name of the fundamental tone in a chord, and the chord is said to be in root-position if the fundamental occurs in the lowest part.

SCALE-DEGREES: Following is a list of the names applied to the degrees of the major scale:

First tone of scale:	Tonic
Second tone of scale:	Supertonic
Third tone of scale:	Mediant
Fourth tone of scale:	Subdominant

Fifth tone of scale:	Dominant
Sixth tone of scale:	Submediant
Seventh tone of scale:	Leading-tone

SEVENTH CHORD: A chord in which the outside interval is a seventh.

TRIAD: A chord formed of three tones in root-position.

(For definitions of the terms "major," "minor," "augmented," "diminished," and "perfect," see table under INTERVAL.)

A
NOTE
ON THE
TYPE IN
WHICH THIS
BOOK IS SET

---

*This book is set
on the Linotype in
Granjon, a type which is
neither a copy of a classic
face nor an original creation.
George W. Jones drew the
basic design for this type from
classic sources, but deviated from
his model wherever four centuries of
type-cutting experience indicated an im-
provement or where modern methods of
punch-cutting made possible a refinement
that was beyond the skill of the sixteenth-
century originator. This new creation is based
primarily upon the type used by Claude Garamond
(1510–1561) in his beautiful French books and
more closely resembles the work of the founder
of the Old Style letter than do any of the various modern-day types that bear his name.*

SET UP, ELECTROTYPED, PRINTED
AND BOUND BY VAIL-BALLOU
PRESS, INC., BINGHAMTON,
N. Y. PAPER MADE BY TICON-
DEROGA PULP & PAPER
CO., TICONDEROGA, N. Y.

Notes on the text

In general, Cowell's text has been left to speak for itself. Readers who are reasonably familiar with the development of Western music will be able to detect for themselves the inconsistencies and eccentricities of some of Cowell's arguments.

For definitions of terms (including those on pages 141–144) and other information, consult The New Harvard Dictionary of Music, ed. Don Michael Randel (Cambridge, MA: The Belknap Press of Harvard University Press, 1986) (henceforth Harvard) and The New Grove Dictionary of Music and Musicians, ed. Stanley Sadie (London: Macmillan Publishers Ltd., 1980) (henceforth Grove).

The following notes are therefore intended mainly to clarify certain topics which readers may be less familiar with (and which are not discussed in the following essay on *New Musical Resources*); to direct readers towards articles in *Harvard* and *Grove* which may be of particular interest; and to provide precise citation of the sources to which Cowell refers.

PAGE/LINE

ix/11 John Redfield, *Music: a Science and an Art* (New York: Alfred A. Knopf, Inc., 1926).

ix/15 Arnold Schoenberg, *Harmonielehre* (Vienna: Universal Edition, 1911); Eng. edn., *Theory of Harmony*, trans. Roy E. Carter (London: Faber and Faber Ltd., 1978).

ix/21 Schoenberg's "later theory . . . as yet unpublished" may be some early incarnation of the 1941 essay "Composition with Twelve Tones (1)" in Arnold Schoenberg, *Style and Idea*, ed. Erwin Stein (London: Faber and Faber Ltd.,

146

1975), 214–245. Certainly, there is a two-page article of the same title dating from 1923: see Josef Rufer, *The Works of Arnold Schoenberg*, trans. Dika Newlin (London: Faber and Faber Ltd., 1962), 165 item 10. Given that the present "Introduction" was written in 1929, information regarding the unpublished theory could have come from Schoenberg's pupil Adolph Weiss – who by this time was secretary of the Pan-American Association of Composers and a close confidant of Cowell's – or possibly at first hand during one of Cowell's European tours.

x/1 A. Eaglefield Hull, *Modern Harmony: its Explanation and Application* (London: Augener Ltd., 1914).

xiv/7–8 Cowell's remarks regarding Javanese and Siamese (Thai) music are not entirely accurate. In Javanese music there are two tunings, slendro and pelog. The former is pentatonic; the latter, like most Thai music, is heptatonic. Neither slendro nor pelog divides the octave into equal parts, though the Thai heptatonic scale does (in theory, if not in practice). See William P. Malm, *Music Cultures of the Pacific, the Near East and Asia*, 2nd edn. (Eaglewood Cliffs, NJ: Prentice–Hall, Inc., 1977), 45–47, 119–123.

xiv/14 For Hába's work with, and writings on, quarter-tones, see Jirí Vyslouzil, "Hába, Alois," *Grove*, VIII: 5–8.

5/1–3 Dayton C. Miller, *The Science of Musical Sounds* (New York: The Macmillan Company, 1916).

8/chart For an explanation of the parentheses around the B–flat in the second column, see the rubric to the corresponding chart on page 11.

12/7 For Greek music, see "Greece. I," *Harvard*, 346–351.

12/13–15 For further information, see – for instance – (1) "Folk music," *Harvard*, 315–319; (2) "Mode," *Harvard*, 499–502

and associated entries; (3) "Plainsong," *Harvard*, 641 and
associated entries.

18/6　See Hugh Davies, "Termen, Lev (Sergeyevich)," *The
　　　New Grove Dictionary of Musical Instruments*, ed. Stanley
　　　Sadie (London: Macmillan Press Ltd., 1984), III: 568–569.

18/20-25　For a general discussion, see (1) "Quarter-tone," *Grove*,
　　　xv: 498; (2) "Microtone," *Harvard*, 491–492. See also (1)
　　　Detlef Gojowy, "Rimsky-Korsakov, Georgy
　　　Mikhaylovich," *Grove*, xvi: 27; (2) Charles Ives, "Some
　　　'Quarter-tone' Impressions," *Essays before a Sonata and
　　　Other Writings*, ed. Howard Boatwright (London: Calder
　　　and Boyars Ltd., 1969), 105–119; (3) Vyslouzil, "Hába,
　　　Alois."

21/29　See "Garbuzov, Nikolai Aleksandrovich," *Great Soviet
　　　Encyclopedia*, trans. of 3rd edn. (New York: Macmillan,
　　　Inc., 1975), VI: 91–92. The theory of undertones, as dis-
　　　cussed in *New Musical Resources*, is very open to question,
　　　though the concept may be related to such other phenom-
　　　ena as sympathetic vibration, difference tones, residue
　　　tones, etc. See (1) Charles Taylor, "Sound, §9: Tones in
　　　sequence and combination," *Grove*, xvii: 560–562; (2)
　　　"Combination tone," *Harvard*, 180–181. In Cowell's man-
　　　uscript text – here called [1919T] – the rather shorter cov-
　　　erage of undertones appears in the context of what are
　　　now pages 3 and 4; there is no equivalent to pages 21–24,
　　　etc. – see pages 164–165 below. Cowell's own ideas (as
　　　expressed in both manuscript and book) were shared with
　　　Charles Seeger: see Marilyn J. Ziffrin, "Angels – Two
　　　Views," *The Music Review*, 39 (1968): 184–196 (note on
　　　page 194). The description of Garbuzov's work in *New
　　　Musical Resources* appears to relate to his "zone" theory of

hearing; unfortunately, none of Garbuzov's publications on the subject are available in English. I am grateful to my colleague Rajmil Fischman for his help in investigating these matters.

30/Ex.2 In [1919T], the musical examples have associated rubrics (see pages 158 159 below). Generally, their omission in the book is unimportant; but the inclusion here of those for Examples 2 and 3 on pages 30 and 31 may be useful. Example 2 (page 30) was originally in two parts. Example 2a (omitted from the book) was as shown, with the rubric "Succession of simple intervals, using single tones as units."

Example 2a

Example 2b was musically identical to the present Example 2, its rubric being "Same succession, each tone being made the fundamental of a chord, and these chords used as units, forming polyintervals, or polyharmony. Section 1. Plain: no embellishment. Sec. 2. Mixed: higher unit unembellished, lower unit embellished with chromatic passing tone. Sec. 3. Embellished: both units embellished, the higher (1a) with anticipation-tone, (2a) with chromatic passing-tone, and (3a) with auxiliary

tone; the lower with auxiliary tone." In the example, (1a)
is associated with section 3's d³, (2a) with b-flat², and (3a)
with f² (N.B. c¹ is middle c).

31/Ex.3   Example 3, as printed here, is musically identical with
example 3 in [1919T]. The rubrics are:
"Ex. 3 (a) Canonic opening of ordinary type, using single
tones as units."
"Ex. 3 (b) The same opening, each tone being made the fundamental of a chord, and the chord successions thus formed
used as contrapuntal units, forming counterchord. Section
1. Plain: no embellishment. The movement in the upper
part is a complete chord change, not an embellishment. Sec.
2. Mixed: the two higher units unembellished, the lower
unit embellished with passing-tone. Sec. 3. Embellished:
both units embellished, the higher with diatonic passing-
tone, the lower with chromatic passing-tone."

32/6   See "Bitonality, polytonality," *Harvard*, 97. Cowell's theoretical distinction between polyharmony and polytonality
is finely drawn but entirely justifiable. The practical difference between the two, however, in the works of Richard
Strauss, Prokofiev, Milhaud, etc., is rather more blurred.

41/4   "Schönberg['s] . . . new system of counterpoint" may sim-
ply refer to the "Method of Composing with Twelve
Tones Which are Related Only with One Another"
(Schoenberg, "Composition with Twelve Tones (1),"
218). However, the text published as Arnold Schoenberg,
Preliminary Exercises in Counterpoint, ed. Leonard Stein
(London: Faber and Faber Ltd., 1963) – which was com-
menced in 1936 – had two earlier (brief) incarnations, of
which Cowell may have been aware. See Rufer, *The
Works of Arnold Schoenberg*, 135–136.

45/1 See "Rhythm," *Harvard*, 700–705.

51/6 Cowell is referring to the siren. See also Henry Cowell, "Preface," *Quartet Romantic [and] Quartet Euphometric* (New York: C.F. Peters Corporation, 1974), [v].

55/18 See Israel J. Katz, "Hornbostel, Erich M(oritz) von" (*sic*), *Grove*, VIII: 716–717. Cowell, as the recipient of a Guggenheim Foundation grant, studied with von Hornbostel in Berlin in 1931–32: see Bruce Saylor, "Cowell, Henry (Dixon)," *The New Grove Dictionary of American Music*, ed. H. Wiley Hitchcock and Stanley Sadie (London: Macmillan Publishers Ltd., 1986), I: 520–529.

59/Ex.10 Note that in Examples 10, 11, 12, 13, 14, 16, 18, 26 and 27 some or all of the triangular-shaped note-heads are printed the wrong way up.

60/6 This line should read "... half-note, against one third-note plus one sixth-note;".

61/Ex.13b The note-heads of the ninth-notes in the third measure should be more extended than those of the tenth-notes in the fourth measure (cf. Example 9, on page 58).

78/Ex.20 The first chord of the final measure lacks a sharp sign before the d.

85/8 See "Konius, Georgii Eduarovich" (*sic*), *Great Soviet Encyclopedia*, XIII: 365. Cowell seems to be referring to some aspect of Konius's metrotechtonic theory of musical form, which attempted "to establish a general abstract principle of musical composition for all works of music (the so-called law of balance of temporal values)."

117/Ex.28 The layout of this example only makes complete sense in the context of the discussion on page 120. As it is, Cowell's four "exact equivalents" appear in the order described on pages 117–118 only on the third of the four staves (i.e. that which uses f^1 as the base pitch of its clusters). The order for the "exact equivalents" on the lowest stave (i.e. that using Cowell's chosen base pitch of c^1) is (4) (1) (2) (3).

118/Ex.30 The lower stave only makes sense with a bass clef substituted for the given treble clef.

121/15 The fifth word should be "notated."

121/Ex.32 The cluster notations used in Examples 32–56 are among several types found in Cowell's compositions. See Michael Hicks, "Cowell's Clusters," *The Musical Quarterly*, 77/3 (fall 1993): 428–458 (particularly pages 442–444).

134/Ex.50 In the final measure, the top stave's flat sign is redundant, and the third stave's given pitches (e^1 and g^1) should actually be tied over from the previous measure as c^1 and e^1.

Henry Cowell's "New Musical Resources"

Background

The origins of *New Musical Resources* lie in Henry Cowell's period of study at Berkeley in 1914–17. His education up to that time had been rather unorthodox; as a consequence, he was taken to Berkeley in the fall of 1914 by his father, Harry, in the hope that his remarkable musical talents might find some appropriate outlet. Charles Seeger, then chair of the Music Department at Berkeley, arranged that the seventeen-year-old Cowell should study harmony and counterpoint with E.G. Stricklen and Wallace Sabin respectively. On Thursday afternoons, Cowell and Seeger met to discuss issues in contemporary music.[1] According to Weisgall, it was also agreed that Cowell

1 For further details of Cowell's studies during this broad period, see (1) Michael Hicks, "Cowell's Clusters," *The Musical Quarterly*, 77/3 (fall 1993): 428–458; (2) William Lichtenwanger, "Henry Cowell: Mind over Music," *The Music of Henry Cowell: a Descriptive Catalog* (Brooklyn, NY: Institute for Studies in American Music, 1986), xiii–xxii; (3) Rita H. Mead, *Henry Cowell's New Music, 1925–1936* (Ann Arbor: UMI Research Press, 1981), 17–30; (4) Bruce Saylor, "Cowell, Henry (Dixon)," *The New Grove Dictionary of American Music*, ed. H. Wiley Hitchcock and Stanley Sadie (London: Macmillan Publishers Ltd., 1986), I: 520–529; (5) Charles Seeger, "Henry Cowell," *Magazine of Art*, 33/5 (May 1940): 288–289; 322–333; (6) Adelaide G. Tusler and Ann M. Briegleb, "Reminiscences of an American Musicologist: Charles Seeger" (Los Angeles: University of California at Los Angeles Oral History Program, 1972; unpublished), 99–104; (7) Hugo Weisgall, "The Music of Henry Cowell," *The Musical Quarterly*, 45 (1959): 484–507. Note that the dates given in some of these sources are mutually contradictory. The present text gives the most plausible sequence of events.

should "suspend free composition for a year," though there is little evidence to support this in Lichtenwanger's catalog.[2]

The consensus view is that Cowell started work on *New Musical Resources* in 1916, at Seeger's behest, though the exact reasons vary among sources. Lichtenwanger states that Seeger urged Cowell "to rationalize his manner of playing piano"; Godwin and Weisgall concur that Seeger encouraged Cowell to "systematize his use of musical resources" while simultaneously creating "the initial repertoire embodying his innovations."[3] From approximately October 1916 to January 1917 (again, precise dates vary among sources) Cowell was in New York, where for a short time he was enrolled at the Institute of Musical Art. On his return to California, he and Seeger continued their discussions; but the study of harmony and counterpoint was replaced by that of written English, undertaken with his old Menlo Park friend and sponsor, Samuel S. Seward Jr. (who was also an English professor at Stanford). Work on *New Musical Resources* intensified, both during the time Cowell and Seward spent in army service at Camp Crane, Pennsylvania, and subsequently.[4] Seward's importance to the project was stressed by

2 Weisgall, "The Music of Henry Cowell," 487. We may assume that the lost *Minuetto* (Nov. 1914) (L128) predated Cowell's first meeting with Seeger: see David Nicholls, *American Experimental Music, 1890–1940* (Cambridge: Cambridge University Press, 1990), 134, 225. Lichtenwanger, *The Music of Henry Cowell*, lists twenty-seven works from the remainder of 1914, thirty-one works for 1915, and twenty-eight works for 1916.

3 (1) Lichtenwanger, *The Music of Henry Cowell*, xxvii; (2) Henry Cowell, *New Musical Resources* (reprint, with a preface and notes by Joscelyn Godwin, New York: Something Else Press, Inc., 1969), xi–xii; (3) Weisgall, "The Music of Henry Cowell," 487.

4 Hicks, "Cowell's Clusters," 444–445.

Cowell in his original (unpublished) introduction to the book (see page 163) as well as in the new introduction he wrote in 1929, prior to publication. Indeed, in 1962 Seward's wife – Amy – recalled that she had spent 1919, the year of their courtship, in competition with *New Musical Resources*.[5]

It is not clear at what stage *New Musical Resources* was typed up. If Cowell was indeed referring to the book in 1922 as "The Unexplored Resources in Musical Effects," then the typed manuscript of the first version – which is clearly headed "New Musical Resources" – must be of a later vintage.[6] Godwin states quite categorically that it was only in 1928 that Cowell – having decided to get the book published – had the manuscript "typed out, reproduced in mauve ink on a spirit duplicator, and sent the rounds of likely publishers."[7] This description of the physical state of the first version is accurate (see page 157) but there is no manuscript evidence either for the date Godwin specifies, or for the response from Knopf (dated 29 January 1929) which he cites. The latter apparently offered publication, provided that Cowell found "a subsidy for 500 copies and will exempt the first thousand ... from royalty."[8] However, Godwin's subsequent assertion –

5 Amy Seward's remark is quoted by Sidney Cowell in a handwritten note contained in [Folder 5] of the manuscript materials for *New Musical Resources* (see below). The note is paraphrased by Godwin on page x of his "Preface" to the 1969 reprint of the book.
6 Hicks ("Cowell's Clusters," 445) cites one source which, as late as July 1922, gave this alternative title to the book. The title does not, however, appear in any of the manuscript materials.
7 Godwin, "Preface," x.
8 Godwin, "Preface," x. The letter from Knopf, and the information regarding the typing and duplication of the manuscript in 1928, were not found among those *New Musical Resources* materials which were available for consultation.

that Cowell immediately started contacting potential purchasers
– is supported by a number of letters written around February
1929. By 7 November, the book (now much revised, as detailed
on pages 162–169) was at the proof stage.

   New Musical Resources was published by Alfred A. Knopf,
Inc., early in 1930 and – according to Godwin – reprinted shortly
afterwards. The book was remaindered in 1935 and the original
plates destroyed in 1942.[9] A reprint was issued in 1969, as
detailed in note 3.

Extant manuscript materials

The manuscript materials relating to *New Musical Resources* are
held in a single box, containing six unnumbered folders whose
contents are as detailed below.[10]

9 Godwin, "Preface," xi. Again, there is no evidence for these state-
   ments among those *New Musical Resources* materials which were
   available for consultation.
10 With the exception of his music manuscripts, all of Cowell's papers
   are housed in the Cowell Collection, Music Division, New York
   Public Library for the Performing Arts. Access to the collection is
   currently restricted and I was allowed access only to the single box
   marked "Cowell Coll. // vi / Box 1 // By HC (Books) // New Musical
   Resources." As is detailed below, the box contains a number of items
   which belong elsewhere in the collection; there is thus every reason to
   assume that materials relating to *New Musical Resources* may be misplaced in other boxes. Until access to the collection is normalized, and
   the collection is properly cataloged, no definitive account of the genesis
   of *New Musical Resources* can be given.
   The "New Musical Resources" box contains six unnumbered folders;
   their ordering and numbering as given here was determined simply
   by the folders' relative positions in the box on 13–15 April 1994 and
   1–4 April 1995.

[Folder 1]

Two sets of galley proofs for the 1930 printing, here called [1930Pi] and [1930Pii].

i [1930Pi] has attached a note from the publisher dated 7 November 1929. Markings are mainly by the copy-editor (usually in green or blue pencil). Cowell's answers to specific queries are in black pencil; he also made a few very minor alterations to the text, usually of punctuation. Music examples are laid in, either pinned or glued to the proofs; some were only set in their final form after the proof stage. This set (and especially its music examples) is in a fragile state.

ii [1930Pii] appears to be from a slightly later stage, and for internal use only; an incomplete note attached to the first sheet indicates that this is the set of page proofs. Diagrams are printed and in place; some music examples are entirely absent. Markings are not in Cowell's hand, and relate to copy-editing and printing matters.

[Folder 2]

Two (spirit duplicated) sets of the original typescript, here called [1919T]. [1919Ti] (discussed here) is the more complete of the two sets: it consists of forty-one typed pages and includes music examples. On page 1, in the top left-hand corner, Sidney Cowell has written, in pencil: "[This draft prior to revision for publication – SRC]."

Substantial differences exist between [1919T] and the published version of the text, here called [1930]. These differences are discussed on pages 162–169.

[Folder 3]

Miscellaneous sheets, here called [1919M], relating to [1919T]; plus one misplaced item.[11]

i three sheets [1919Mi–iii] each having handwritten music examples, in black ink, glued on. The examples are numbered 1, 2a, 2b, 3a, 3b, 4, 5, 6, 7.

2a and 4 do not appear in [1930].

ii a single sheet of music paper [1919Miv], approximately 4″ x 1″, written in black ink, with typed rubric "Fig. 35." This equates to Example 48 in [1930].

iii four variously sized sheets [1919Mv–viii] of typed rubrics for examples, as follows:

[1919Mv] rubrics for examples 2b, 3b.

[1919Mvi] rubrics for examples 10a, 10b, 14, 15, 17.

[1919Mvii] rubrics for examples 6, 6 (with longer text), 7, 10a, 10b, 14, 15, 17.

[1919Mviii] duplicate of [1919Mvii].

[Folder 4]

Similar materials to those in [Folder 3] but in far greater quantities [1919Mix–x]; plus one misplaced item.[12]

11 The misplaced item is a single typed page (numbered 8) on the work of Paul Creston.

12 The misplaced item is a tiny fragment of a typed letter which appears to have no relevance to *New Musical Resources*.
Between them, [Folder 3] and [Folder 4] contain a complete set of rubrics for [1919T], but eight of the examples are missing. However, [1919Ti] itself contains a complete set of examples and rubrics: the former are handwritten in black (or occasionally blue) ink and pasted onto regularly sized sheets, accompanied by the corresponding rubrics. Four of [1919T]'s examples do not reappear in [1930]; conversely, nine of [1930]'s fifty-six examples are not found in [1919T].

i [1919MIX] a large number of handwritten music examples, in black ink; some are already cut; others are on larger sheets containing one or more examples; most have typed identifiers (e.g. "Fig. 8.") or rubrics.

ii [1919MX] a large number of typed rubrics for the music examples, most in multiple copies (four or more); some are already cut.

[Folder 5]

Various items of correspondence, here called [1930c], mostly relating to the 1930 publication of *New Musical Resources*; plus some misplaced items.[13]

i [1930ci] a handwritten, pencil note by Sidney Cowell, on a manila folder; not dated. Text as follows:

"1st outline begun in 1916

1919 Book finished with much help from SS Seward Jr (all during the year of their courtship says Amy Seward in 1962, she had to compete with that book!)

Revised in presentation and cut in 1929 for publ. [by?]

Knopf that year (or maybe 1930 was publ. date) But no essential change Henry thinks. Parts omitted were loaned to John Cage who preserved them & they are or will be at NYPL

---

13 The order of the items given here is that of their relative positions in [Folder 5] on 13–15 April 1994 and 1–4 April 1995. The misplaced items are (1) an incomplete set of lecture notes (in Cowell's hand?) for a lecture on mainly far-eastern music, including indications of where (? recorded) examples would be played; (2) two letters (one each from William Lichtenwanger and Lee Fairley) dated September 1950, inviting Cowell to review items for *Notes*; (3) a letter from *The Musical Quarterly*, dated 1951, accompanying payment for a "Current Chronicle" article by Cowell of January 1951.

with other Cowell papers & mss. & proofs of the published
book."

ii [1930cii] four flyers from Knopf, printed black on gray
paper; not dated. The announcement of *New Musical
Resources* is coupled with that of Winthrop Parkhurst's
The Anatomy of Music.

iii [1930ciii] letter addressed to Mr. B.W. Walton, West 68th
St., New York; dated 6 March 1930; sent by Frederick
Hutchins, Registrar of the State Conservatorium of Music,
Sydney, Australia. It acknowledges Walton's letter of 28
January 1930, which had accompanied a copy of *New
Musical Resources*; the copy "has been placed in the
Conservatorium Library . . ."[14]

iv [1930civ] a fragile, handwritten note by Henry Cowell; not
dated. Text summarized as follows:
[side 1] "Pledges Toward Book Publication" lists those who
have pledged to buy copies, the number of copies so pledged,
and whether or not payment has been received. Blanche
Walton took 100 ("Paid"), [Georgia] Kober 25, [Richard]
Buhlig 5, [Mrs. John B.] Casserly 20, [Charles] Ives 5, etc.
The list contains around thirty names and notes that "129
copies, besides Blanche, sent out as sold."[15]
[side 2] appears to be a list of those who had been, or were to
be, asked to pledge; some names duplicate those on [side 1].
Over both sides is a list of over 100 individuals to whom
complimentary copies had been sent.

14 "Mr. B.W. Walton" was in fact Cowell's friend and patron Blanche
Walton, whose importance to *New Musical Resources* is discussed below.

15 One assumes that most of Blanche Walton's 100 copies were sent out
to potentially interested institutions, as is indicated by [1930ciii].

v [1930cv] a selection of letters, apparently responding to
pledge requests from Cowell; some contain pencil annota-
tions by Sidney Cowell; all appear to date from February
1929.

vi [1930cvi] a photocopy of a *Times Literary Supplement* review
of the 1969 reprint of *New Musical Resources*.

[Folder 6]

Typescript toward [1930], here called [1929T]. Sixty-five normal-
sized sheets, being either (new) top copies [1929Tn], or (older)
duplicated sheets [1929To], or some combination of the two; no
music examples, though all the textual references to them are in
place. The top sheet has pinned to it a note relating to the (type)
setting. The typescript is fairly heavily annotated in red ink (?by
the copy-editor, presumably for the typesetter); it also contains
black pencil markings and alterations by Cowell, most of which
occur on the duplicated pages or portions of duplicated pages
(the newly typed pages and portions, in contrast, usually contain
only the marks of the [?copy-editor]). The text *as edited* is that of
[1930]; the vast majority of the editorial corrections are of
spelling, grammar and punctuation.

The [1929To] sections – whether whole pages or less – are taken
directly from another (third) set of [1919T]. These [1929To] sections – often containing changes by Cowell – are interlinked
with, and pasted onto, those of [1929Tn]; generally speaking, the
earlier parts of [1929T] consist of [n] text and the later parts of [o]
text. Apart from the new text contained in the [1929Tn] pages,
also new here are Cowell's "Introduction" and "Definition of
Terms" (see below).

Differences between [1919T] and [1929T]/[1930]

In essence, therefore, there are two distinct versions of *New Musical Resources* – that contained in the earlier duplicated typescript [1919T], and that which was published [1929T]/ [1930]. As was stated earlier, the date of [1919T] cannot be ascertained from the materials currently available: the range of possibilities extends from 1919 to 1928; however, the *textual substance* of [1919T] places it firmly at the earlier end of the range, as will be apparent from the following discussion.

Extant correspondence [1930cv] seems to support Godwin's assertion that Knopf had been approached – and had responded fairly positively – by early 1929; equally, [1930p] can be placed with certainty in November 1929. The original material sent to Knopf must, though, have been [1919T], as the text of [1929T] – for reasons discussed below – could only have been written following Cowell's visit to Russia in May 1929.

In [1930ci] Sidney Cowell suggests that [1930] was "revised in presentation and cut in 1929 . . . But no essential change Henry thinks." Neither half of this statement is entirely accurate, however; for although some relatively short sections of [1919T] were indeed cut, and do not reappear in [1930], the texts which replaced them are invariably more substantial. Furthermore, while the general thrust of Cowell's argument remains the same in both versions of the text, the range of reference in [1930] is far greater and more impressive than in [1919T].

It would be inappropriate to discuss here the myriad minor differences which exist between the two versions of *New Musical Resources*; the substantive differences, though, are detailed below.[16]

16 As has been noted above, the music examples in [1919T] are accompanied by rubrics. In general, these are not referred to in the following discussion.

"INTRODUCTION"

In [1919T] this is titled "Personal Introduction" and consists of three fairly short paragraphs which baldly state Cowell's reasons for writing the book. The last paragraph thanks both Charles Seeger and Samuel Seward for their help; the reference to Seeger as "my friend and former teacher" places the text after 1917, as would be expected.

[1930]'s "Introduction" is entirely new and considerably longer. While its basic function is not dissimilar to that of [1919T], the range of reference to matters both scientific and musical demonstrates the breadth and depth of Cowell's experiences during the intervening period. Indeed, none of the references to individual composers, scientific and musical texts, etc., found here appears in [1919T].[17] Nor does Cowell refer in [1919T] to the "theory of musical relativity" which *New Musical Resources* has now come to embody [1930, pages xi, xvi–xvii in the present edition]. The final paragraph of [1930] still acknowledges Seward's help, but puzzlingly omits any reference to Seeger. There is no obvious explanation for this, lest it be connected with the issue of historical precedence: either Cowell may have been attempting to cover his musical traces, or he and Seeger may have had a disagreement.[18]

17 While we can hardly expect Cowell to have referred in [1919T] to texts that had yet to be written, he also failed to cite A. Eaglefield Hull, *Modern Harmony: its Explanation and Application*, (London: Augener Ltd., 1914). Equally significant, both here and elsewhere in [1919T], is Cowell's apparent lack of knowledge of other contemporary composers and musical trends.

18 In Seeger, "Henry Cowell," on page 288, we read that "[Cowell] swiped many of his best (and some of his worst) 'ideas' from me, and occasionally acknowledges it" (as Cowell had in [1919]). Seeger's remarks regarding autodidactation, found later on the same page, are

"THE INFLUENCE OF OVERTONES IN MUSIC"

In [1919T] this is titled "The Law of Overtones in Past Musical History" and is the first section of Chapter – rather than Part – 1.

A number of passages in [1930] are new, and have no equivalent in [1919T]. These are:

  i page 3/lines 6–17.

 ii page 4/line 6 to page 7/line 10.

   However, a paragraph cut from [1919T] does equate to [1930]'s page 5/lines 1–4. This cut paragraph – which was actually placed on what in [1930] is page 9, between lines 27 and 28 – includes one of [1919T]'s few references to a published text: Dayton C. Miller, *The Science of Musical Sounds*, (New York: The Macmillan Company, 1916).[19]

iii page 11/line 8 (i.e. after the chart) to page 12/line 2.

   The ensuing discussion, as far as page 16/line 18, is far less substantive in [1919T] and includes reference only to the work of Beethoven, Wagner, Debussy and Schoenberg.

iv page 17/lines 5–13 and 17–23.

 v page 18/line 6 to page 23/line 16. Cowell's knowledge of the topics discussed here was gained during the 1920s. In particular, his references to Georgy Rimsky-Korsakov and

also of relevance. Cowell's covering of the traces of his musical development is a strong sub-plot throughout Hicks, "Cowell's Clusters." By 1930, Seeger was beginning to move away from composition and towards (mainly ethno-) musicology. Conversely, he was currently teaching Ruth Crawford composition, while an article on dissonant counterpoint – which parallels (and substantially amplifies) pages 35–42 of *New Musical Resources* – was soon to be published: Charles Seeger, "On Dissonant Counterpoint," *Modern Music*, 7 (June–July, 1930): 25–31. See also Nicholls, *American Experimental Music*, 90–91, 134–141.

19 The title given in [1919T] – and here – is correct; that in [1930] is not.

Nikolai Garbuzov confirm that this new material could only
have been written after his May 1929 visit to Russia.
In addition to these new passages in [1930], it should be noted
that in [1919T] "The Law of Overtones in Past Musical History"
concluded with what is now page 18/line 5. Page 23/line 17 to
page 24/line 6 (including the undertone chart) appear in [1919T]
in the section on "Polyharmony" (see below).

"POLYHARMONY"

In [1919T], page 25/lines 4 and 6 refer to undertones as well as
overtones.

Page 25/line 18 is followed in [1919T] by two sentences referring to Schoenberg's use of the term "polyharmony" in his
Harmonielehre.[20]

[1919T] has no equivalent to [1930]'s page 25/line 19 to page
27/line 10.

In [1919T] some of [1930]'s material is placed differently.
Specifically, [1930]'s page 23/line 17 to page 24/line 6 (including
the undertone chart) appear in the context of what became
[1930]'s page 28, between lines 3 and 4.

The rubrics from [1919T] which accompany [1930]'s
Examples 3 and 4 are given on pages 149–150 of the "Notes on
the text."

[1919T]'s discussion of "Polyharmony" concludes with what
in [1930] is page 32/line 5: the remaining two sentences in [1930]
are new.

---

20 The actual reference in [1919T] is to Schoenberg's "treatise on harmony" which was at this time only available in German, as Arnold
Schoenberg, *Harmonielehre* (Vienna: Universal Edition, 1911).

"TONE-QUALITY"

This section does not appear in [1919T] and was newly written for [1930].

"DISSONANT COUNTERPOINT"

[1919T] and [1930] are effectively identical up to page 40/line 5. [1919T] then concludes with two short paragraphs not present in [1930]: their tone is very much of dissonant counterpoint being a relatively untried technique (which, in 1919 or thereabouts, it was).[21] The considerably longer continuation of [1930] – with its references to music which had been written during the subsequent decade and its citation of composers more recent than Reger and Franck – is consequently rather less defensive in tone.

"RHYTHM [INTRODUCTION]"

[1919T] commences at page 46/line 18: there is no equivalent to [1930]'s preceding material. All other changes are minor, though a reference in [1919T] to Helmholtz – at page 47/line 20 – has been removed.

"TIME"

[1930] contains three passages which have no equivalent in [1919T]:

   i page 55/line 5 to page 56/line 3. The additional material, as is so often the case, expands the frame of reference.

  ii page 57/line 25 to page 59/line 7. The notation chart – given

21 The first paragraph begins "The ultimate test of this music, or of any music written on a new musical basis, is of course the practical one of ultimate acceptability, and that is obviously a question for the future."

as Example 9 in [1930] – is present in [1919T], but Example
10 is not. The new text – including Example 10 – is intended
primarily to amplify further the advantages of the notational
system, as perceived by Cowell.

iii page 62/line 16 to page 66/line 10; [1919T] ends with what in
[1930] is Example 14. [1930]'s references to the player-piano
and to the mechanical instrument described on pages 65–66
are discussed below, on pages 173 and 171 respectively.

"METRE"

The only new text in [1930] occurs between page 69/line 13 and
page 71/line 18.

Additionally, [1930]'s Example 17 (and the preceding reference to it on page 72) are not present in [1919T].

"DYNAMICS" AND "FORM"

These sections do not appear in [1919T] and were newly written
for [1930]. The reference on page 85 to Georgii Konius further
demonstrates that this new material could only have been written following Cowell's May 1929 visit to Russia.

"METRE AND TIME COMBINATIONS"

The texts of [1919T] and [1930] are effectively identical.

"TEMPO"

The only significant difference is the addition in [1930] of a new
paragraph from page 93/line 10 (i.e. after Example 24) to page
94/line 2.

"SCALES OF RHYTHM"

[1919T] and [1930] are effectively identical, but for the following exceptions:

i [1919T] has a more extensive introduction than [1930]; the cut text, constituting approximately half of one typed page, was originally placed on page 98 between lines 21 and 22.

ii the sentence in [1930] on page 104 (lines 15–17) concerning the player-piano is not found in [1919T].

iii this section of [1919T] finishes at page 108/line 2. The text from "or the..." onwards – with its references to Chopin, Stravinsky, Ives et al. – is new in [1930].

"BUILDING CHORDS FROM DIFFERENT INTERVALS"

This section does not appear in [1919T] and was newly written for [1930]. Consequently, [1930]'s overall title for Part III – "Chord Formation" – is also new.

"TONE-CLUSTERS"

[1919T] starts quite differently from [1930]: the two versions only come together at page 121/line 3. Thus [1930]'s page 117/line 1 to page 121/line 2 are new.

The corresponding material excised from [1919T] consists of five paragraphs which together fill less than one typed page. In this excised material, Cowell refers to Schoenberg and Ornstein; given the importance of both composers (and especially the latter) to the development of tone clusters – and Cowell's own later attempts to establish his historical precedence in this area – this is a significant revision. [22]

22 On Cowell, Ornstein, Schoenberg and the development of the tone cluster, see Hicks, "Cowell's Clusters," 437–440, 451–452.

The following minor additions appear in [1930]:

i page 121/lines 14–18, as well as the two parts of Example 32 that surround them. In fact, this originally constituted the two parts of [1919]'s example 18; the text was the rubric to (b). The example appears in the third of the five excised paragraphs referred to above.

ii page 125/lines 6–7.

From page 136/line 5 (i.e. after [1930]'s "(See Example 54.)") the two versions again go their separate ways. [1919T] includes a short discussion of what might be termed tonality-based clusters, which is replaced in [1930] by the text running from page 136/line 5 to page 137/line 11. The remainder of [1930] is a substantial reworking of the brief, and rather more hesitant, final paragraph of [1919T].

"DEFINITIONS OF TERMS"

This material does not appear in [1919T] and was newly written for [1930].

"New Musical Resources" and the music of its own time

Given that Cowell probably wrote *New Musical Resources* out of "the necessity to systematize his use of musical resources," while simultaneously creating "the initial repertoire embodying his innovations," strong links between the "theory of musical relativity" and his music are easily established.[23] The only complicating factor is that while [1919T]'s text is fully coterminous with

---

23 (1) Godwin, "Preface," xi–xii; (2) Weisgall, "The Music of Henry Cowell," 487.

Cowell's works of the period 1916–19, that of [1930] both views those earlier works with the benefit of hindsight and adds a new layer of commentary on pieces composed during the intervening decade.

Not all the techniques discussed in *New Musical Resources* found practical expression in Cowell's music. He only occasionally uses polyharmony and sliding tones, for instance, while a number of ideas – including the ordering of tempi and dynamics – are seemingly never taken up. In other cases, however, theory and practice are inextricably linked. Thus an early form of dissonant counterpoint – which had itself originally been devised by Charles Seeger in connection with his teaching of Cowell – underlies many pieces from the 1910s and 1920s. These include the String Quartet No.1 (Apr. 1916)(L197), the string quintet *Ensemble* (1924)(L380), the *Seven Paragraphs* for string trio (1925)(L408), and the Movement for String Quartet (1928)(L450). Similarly, the rhythmic and metric complexities of the *Quartet Romantic* (Sep. 1917)(L223), *Quartet Euphometric* (Sep.1919)(L283), and the piano work *Fabric* (Sep. 1920)(L307) are explained in *New Musical Resources* in the sections on "Time" and "Metre" (pages 49–66 and 66–81 respectively). Cowell's use of tone clusters (which are discussed in the book's final chapter) is well known: indeed, cluster-dominated works such as *Dynamic Motion* (Nov. 1916)(L213/1) and *The Tides of Manaunaun* (Jul. 1917)(L219/1) are among his most popular. It might be noted, incidentally, that Cowell's use of many of these techniques was not curtailed by the publication of *New Musical Resources*, but rather that he continued to employ them after 1930.[24]

24 For a much fuller discussion of the links between *New Musical Resources* and Cowell's music written before 1940, see Nicholls, *American Experimental Music*, 134–159.

There are also a relatively small number of instances of Cowell taking up for the first time in his post–1930 work ideas which had been mooted in *New Musical Resources*. On pages 65–66, Cowell describes an "instrument . . . which would mechanically produce a rhythmic ratio, but which would be controlled by hand." Such an instrument – which he called the rhythmicon – was built for Cowell in 1931, by Lev Termen. Although Cowell seems originally to have conceived of the rhythmicon as – in Lichtenwanger's words – "merely a highly sophisticated metronome" he also wrote at least two pieces for it – the Concerto for rhythmicon and orchestra (Nov. 1931)(L481) and the lost [Music for violin and rhythmicon] (May 1932)(L485).[25] In another, more general, sense Cowell seems to have followed his own advice regarding form (pages 84–85). Before 1930, Cowell's music tends not to exhibit sophistication of formal construction; but in a series of pieces from 1934 onwards – including *Ostinato Pianissimo* (1934)(L505), the *United Quartet* (1936)(L522), and *Pulse* (May 1939)(L565) – he explores the organization of form through means which (while not in any apparent way relating to the metrical harmonies suggested in *New Musical Resources*) certainly "make for perfection of outline, and . . . give a clarity and purpose to the composition as a whole, which are often lacking in works using experimental material" (page 84). Somewhat paradoxically, during the same period he also continued with the (diametrically opposed) exploration of variable form first suggested in *Anger Dance* (May 1914)(L104/6).[26]

25 Lichtenwanger, *The Music of Henry Cowell*, xxix, 132, 135. See also Henry Cowell, "Preface," *Quartet Romantic [and] Quartet Euphometric* (New York: C.F. Peters Corporation, 1974), [v]; here Cowell suggests that discussions with Termen may have taken place as early as 1929.

26 See Nicholls, *American Experimental Music*, 167–174, for a discussion of Cowell's various formal experiments of this period.

As well as aiding our understanding of Cowell's music, some of the ideas discussed in *New Musical Resources* also have relevance to the music of several of his contemporaries. Dissonant counterpoint, as mentioned earlier, was first devised by Charles Seeger in the late 1910s, at least partly in connection with his teaching of Cowell. Examples of pieces written within its disciplines include not only many works by Cowell, but also pieces by Seeger, Carl Ruggles, John J. Becker, Lou Harrison and – most importantly – Ruth Crawford. Cowell partially describes Ruggles's compositional practice on pages 41–42 of *New Musical Resources*, while Seeger's discussion of both Ruggles and Crawford is found in Cowell's later compilation *American Composers on American Music*.[27] Similarly, tone clusters are found not only in Cowell's work, but also – in differing ways – in that of Ives, Ornstein, Schoenberg, and Crawford, to name but four. And, as the text of [1930] makes clear, there are other techniques discussed in *New Musical Resources* which also have resonances in the music of Cowell's contemporaries.

"New Musical Resources" and the music of more recent times

Although the "theory of musical relativity" has never been taken fully on board by any composer – including Cowell himself – both *New Musical Resources* and many of the individual ideas

27 Henry Cowell, ed., *American Composers on American Music* (Stanford: Stanford University Press, 1933; New York: Frederick Ungar Publishing Co., Inc., 1962). Ruggles and Crawford are discussed in chapters II and XVII respectively. Cowell's estimation of Seeger appears as chapter XVIII. See also Nicholls, *American Experimental Music*, 89–140, for a discussion of the dissemination of dissonant counterpoint.

contained within it have continued to influence modernist thought, either overtly or covertly. Indeed, in some instances what might to Cowell have seemed throwaway remarks have been taken surprisingly seriously. The most obvious example of this is the mature work of Conlon Nancarrow, which is directly attributable to Cowell's suggestion (on pages 64–65) that while "Some of the rhythms developed through the present acoustical investigation could not be played by any living performer . . . [they] could easily be cut on a player-piano roll." Equally, sliding tones and natural sounds (pages 19–21) have been of enormous importance – either conceptually or compositionally – to several composers, including La Monte Young and Iannis Xenakis.

Cowell's thoughts on tempo (pages 90–98) anticipated a number of innovations in post-war music, including Elliott Carter's metric modulation, and the temporal complexities of both Cage – in the *Music of Changes* (1951) and elsewhere – and his European contemporaries. Interestingly, the *Music of Changes* was one of Cage's last works to employ the so-called "square-root form" which had been the basis of his compositional technique since 1939. "Square-root form" had itself been derived from those mid–1930s formal procedures of Cowell's mentioned earlier. After reaching its apogee in the music of Ruth Crawford, dissonant counterpoint *per se* has slowly disappeared from common usage. But tone clusters have proved to be a resilient and robust resource: volume 5 of *Die Reihe* contains an extended essay on their possibilities, while composers as different in outlook as Lou Harrison, Xenakis and Frederick Rzewski have recently employed clusters in their works.[28] Perhaps the final words on the continuing importance of *New*

28 Mauricio Kagel, "Tone-clusters, Attacks, Transitions," *Die Reihe*, 5 (1959): 40–55.

Musical Resources should come from Mauricio Kagel. In "Tone-clusters, Attacks, Transitions," Kagel praised Cowell's book for being "one of the few documents to treat concretely and shrewdly the ideas about musical theory developed during the first half of the twentieth century ... we return to [its experiments] not in order to discover an unknown method but to show that, even today, Cowell's reasoning can be reconciled with the newest problem of serial music ... His book is therefore a document whose theoretical approach, still relevant forty years after it was written, illuminated aspects of technique, while not burdening itself with outmoded aesthetic demands." [29] A further forty years on, Kagel's view of *New Musical Resources* is still entirely apposite.

29 Kagel, "Tone-clusters, Attacks, Transitions," 40–41.

Index